The Motley Fool's
GUIDE TO

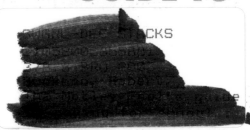

PAYING FOR SCHOOL

*how to cover **education** costs from **K** to **Ph.D.***

WITHDRAWN

ROBERT BROKAMP
FOREWORD BY TOM GARDNER

Published by The Motley Fool, Inc., 123 North Pitt Street,
Alexandria, Virginia, 22314, USA

First Printing, January 2003
10 9 8 7 6 5 4 3 2 1

ISBN 1-892547-26-0

Printed in the United States of America
Body set in ITC Veljovic 11/15. Titling set in Futura and Veljovic.

Distributed by Publishers Group West

Cover design by Richard Engdahl
Interior Design by Pneuma Books, LLC
For more information, visit www.pneumabooks.com

Printed by United Book Press, Inc.

The Motley Fool

The Motley Fool's mission is to educate, amuse, and enrich. Begun as a newsletter serving 60 readers in August 1994, the Fool now reaches millions of people each month and is a leading provider of financial education and independent advice. It serves to help people achieve financial independence across a wide variety of online and offline media channels, including its award-winning website at www.Fool.com, its best-selling Simon & Schuster and self-published books, a nationally syndicated weekly newspaper column carried by more than 200 publications, and "The Motley Fool Radio Show," a joint venture with NPR.

WHAT IS FOOLISHNESS?

Keep in mind as you read this book that, to us, "Foolish" is a positive adjective. The Motley Fool takes its name from Shakespeare. In Elizabethan drama, the Fool is usually the one who can tell the king the truth without losing his head—literally. We Fools aim to tell you the truth, too—that you can learn enough about money and investing to build a secure financial future for yourself. To learn more about The Motley Fool, drop by our website at www.Fool.com or on America Online at keyword: FOOL.

About the Author

As a former financial advisor and English teacher, it was inevitable that Robert Brokamp would one day write about the management of money. His musings on retirement, investments, budgeting, and other topics can be found on Fool.com, in The Motley Fool's syndicated newspaper column, in *The Motley Fool Personal Finance Workbook*, as well as on other media outlets such as *Newsweek* magazine and Fox television.

Acknowledgments

Writing a book is like giving birth, with many people cheering, "Breathe! Breathe! Push! Push! Ewwww!"

Among the noteworthy midwives who assisted in the delivery of this book are Dayana Yochim, Selena Maranjian, and Bob Bobala, whose feedback and camaraderie are unparalleled. As is the case with any Fool tome, Alissa Territo did an outstanding job of monitoring development, from conception to creation. Many, many thanks to Roy Lewis for answering an onslaught of tax questions, and to Rick Engdahl for his splendid work on the cover. Mounds of chocolatey gratitude are to be heaped upon Reggie Santiago, the editor of this guide, who had to read it several times. My condolences.

I am timelessly grateful to my wife, Elizabeth, for her mighty support. Finally, I must thank my high school English teacher, Anita Huenke, for making my education so valuable.

*To my parents, Elaine and Frank, who made
my education a priority.*

Table of Contents

Foreword

For years, the mission of The Motley Fool has been to educate, to amuse, and to enrich. Whatever our subject—money, health, technology, family life—our aims are always 1) to learn something together, 2) to generate wealth, vibrancy, and plenty from all our endeavors, and 3) to share a laugh along the way. Following through on those promises makes life a little easier, a little more pleasant. In fact, it's this triangle of our mission that has attracted such talented writers (like the author of this book) and such a creative, interesting, and warm audience (that's you—take a bow).

Now, if I had to narrow our mission down to just one of these, it'd be hard not to hold onto sharing a good laugh together. We live in a world that is sometimes dreadfully and unnecessarily serious. I just walked through a Polo Ralph Lauren store, swept in 30%-off signs in the wake of Christmas. Nice clothes, I thought. But look how serious everyone is. Nice shirts, nice shoes, but where's the wink and the nod and the play? I guess it's not in their mission statement. I'd find it hard to imagine a Motley Fool without the glint of humor in her eye.

It would likewise be difficult to set aside enrichment as an aim. Among the riches to celebrate, we cheer emotional, spiritual, intellectual, and material wealth. I'd hate to think anyone would visit our website without getting a taste of each. Emotional riches for those using our service to quit smoking or fight cancer. Spiritual wealth in the dazzling community discussions among Fools of all faiths. Intellectual nourishment during an interview with the CEO of Starbucks or Whole Foods or a talk with George Foreman on our NPR radio program. And material gains when we Fools work together to negotiate effectively in the car lots, insurance houses, and brokerage firms of America.

It would be tough to let go of humor and enrichment at The Motley Fool.

Yet, I'd set both aside in order to preserve our attempts "to educate." We deal today primarily in a subject that gets the cold shoulder in our nation's high schools and universities. None to teach us about credit card debt. None to explain whole-life versus term insurance. None to calculate the timeless miracle of compound growth made widely available via index mutual funds. None to point us toward saving and away from overspending.

The Motley Fool could never let go of this, our primary aim: teaching and learning together. We would be very little in the end if all we did was make you laugh and throw hot stock ticker symbols at you. This whole adventurous experiment we've been running for a decade would bubble and shatter like mishandled test tubes if we failed to teach you much of anything along the way.

Thankfully, our mission need not be narrowed. But within it, please know how enthusiastic we are about learning important subjects together. If you are an avid reader of ours, I suspect you know that. If not, you are about to encounter one of our most Foolish writers. Robert Brokamp is a wonderful, practical, and just plain fun writer (he's not a bad guy, either). He carries out our mission beautifully. He will teach you, entertain you, and save you money in your pursuit of education. He will explain how the business of education is run, help you find aid and save money on tuition, and win a few laughs along the way.

Enjoy it.

—Tom Gardner, co-founder of The Motley Fool
December 31, 2002

Introduction

The roots of education are bitter, but the
fruit is sweet.   —Aristotle

Most people assume that Aristotle was commenting on the effort required to achieve an education. But he was actually reacting to the rising cost of tuition at Plato's Academy and the baffling financial aid application process.

Not really. But if you look at the price of attending school today—whether it's a private elementary or secondary school, an undergraduate program, or graduate school—you can't help but feel sour in the stomach.

Still, as Aristotle suggested, the payoff is sweet. Looking just at the financial rewards, the average college graduate earns 80 percent more than the average high school grad, according to the Census Bureau. Over the course of their careers, that earnings gap widens as workers with higher levels of education pull in even larger paychecks.

Of course, an education means more than a better salary. How can you assign a dollar amount to the broadened intellect, heightened curiosity, expanded opportunities, sharper communication skills, and body piercings that might result from attending the right school?

EARNINGS BASED ON EDUCATION LEVEL

Level of education	Lifetime earnings (in 1999 dollars)
High school graduate	$1.2 million
Bachelor's degree	$2.1 million
Master's degree	$2.5 million
Professional degree	$4.4 million
School of hard knocks	Priceless

But it's still reassuring to know that an education is an investment with great potential. Our aim is to make the bitter price of an education easier to swallow. With this Foolish guide in hand and resolve in your heart, here are some of the money-saving tactics you'll learn:

WHERE TO PUT YOUR SCHOOL-RELATED SAVINGS

Over the past 10 to 15 years, burgeoning tuition costs have been accompanied by new ways to save for those costs. Coverdell Education Savings Accounts, prepaid tuition plans, and 529 savings accounts are some of the most recent and prominent that offer exceptional tax advantages, but each in its own way. Plus, they have different effects on financial aid eligibility. You'll learn which account is best for you.

HOW TO GET THE MOST FINANCIAL AID

All you have to do is complete the FAFSA—and perhaps the PROFILE—to determine your EFC and thus your SAR, making sure to XYZPDQ. We'll take you through the process, step by step, complete with translation. You *can* increase the chances that you'll get a piece of the $90 billion financial aid pie, even if you make a decent living.

HOW TO CUT THE COSTS OF EDUCATION

Don't let the price tag on a diploma scare you. There are ways to get a deal, from winning scholarships, to finding employers and government agencies willing to foot the bill, to taking general electives at cheaper schools, to buying used textbooks.

HOW TO INVEST FOR SCHOOL

Welcome to Money Management 101. You'll learn the differences between stocks, bonds, and cash equivalents, and where your money should be throughout the college-saving adventure.

HOW EDUCATION COSTS CAN REDUCE YOUR TAXES

Uncle Sam wants you to be able to afford an education. He's not just being avuncular—he knows that an educated citizenry is a tax revenue-generating citizenry. Accordingly, he has established a host of ways to offset tuition bills with tax deductions and credits.

Put it all together, and you can save thousands of dollars. In fact, for people who do the necessary preparation, demonstrate the right skills, and find the right circumstances, an education can be downright cheap. It takes just two things: information and action. We'll provide the former, and outline a plan that points you in the direction of the latter.

YOUR OTHER FINANCIAL PRIORITIES

Paying for school is an important goal, but it's only part of a broader financial plan. While developing your saving-for-school strategy, keep these other priorities in mind:

- **Pay off high-interest debt:** It doesn't make sense to earn 4 to 10 percent on your college savings when you're paying 11 to 20 percent on your credit card debt. If you owe more than $500 on any loan that charges double-digit interest, pay that off first.

- **Build an emergency fund:** You need a stash of accessible cash available to extinguish the potential hazards of unexpected expenses. If you don't have the money available when the furnace blows up, the roof falls in, or your department gets "downsized," then you'll have to turn to the credit card, retirement fund, or college cookie jar. This is not good. Keep three to six months' worth of expenses in a money market investment.

- **Get adequately insured:** Purchase a 10- or 20-year term life insurance policy to replace the income (or child-rearing and home-keeping services) of any members of the family who join that great frat party in the sky. Also, look into disability insurance since it is more likely that a worker will be temporarily out of work (due to an injury or illness) than permanently (due to kicking the bucket).

- **Save for retirement:** Do not sacrifice retirement savings for college savings. If you don't have enough to cover tuition, your student can apply for financial aid and borrow money. However, there are no scholarships or loans for retirees. If you haven't saved enough to retire, then you can't.

Five Fast Facts

1. The No. 1 source of information on financial aid for a private elementary or secondary education is the school itself. Most aid comes directly from the school, and it will also be a good source of leads for outside aid.

2. There isn't one book or website that lists aid available for private schooling. You'll have to do some scholarship snooping. Use the Internet, ask your employer, and investigate whether money is available from organizations to which you're affiliated.

3. If you are setting aside money for private school, a Coverdell Education Savings Account is a good place to put it. The money grows tax-free, and can be used for anything from tuition to uniforms to computers.

4. Another place for money earmarked for education is a custodial account, commonly known as an UGMA or UTMA (depending on your state). The first $750 in earnings are tax-free, and the next $750 are taxed at 10 percent. After that, earnings are taxed at the parents' income bracket.

5. You can borrow money for a private education, but only do so for a year or two. Otherwise, you'll be borrowing every year... and then come college costs! That'll be a heckuva debt dungeon from which to escape.

Chapter 1

Paying for Private Elementary or Secondary School

In this chapter...
- The costs of a private education
- Financial aid
- Tax-friendly savings accounts
- Other sources of aid
- Money-saving tips

Parents send their kids to private elementary and secondary schools for many reasons, such as good programs or smaller class sizes. They might also want their children to receive a religion-based education, or are of the opinion that their local public school stinks. Or they think their tykes look darling in plaid jumpers or knickers.

Whatever the reasons, a lot of parents are convinced. According to the National Center for Education Statistics, there were 5.3 million students enrolled in 27,000 pri-

TAKE IT FROM SOMEONE WHO KNOWS

Who better to offer perspective on paying for a private education than someone who has done it, and now works in the system? Karen Nerrie and her husband Jim provided private educations for their three children, and she is now the director of development at a parochial high school in Anaheim, Calif. Her advice:

Affording private school for your children must be a priority. If you approach it with this frame of mind, you will find ways to make it happen.

My husband and I chose to forego other things in favor of paying tuition. We used coupons at the grocery store, cooked homemade food instead of eating out, shopped sales, and did not go on expensive vacations. You would be surprised how much that can save.

Plan for tuition early on, just like college tuition. We noticed that college tuition seemed much less shocking because we had paid tuition beginning in kindergarten; it was just another jump up for us.

In my opinion, an excellent college-prep education at a private school is the best way to increase your chances of being awarded college merit scholarships. Each of our three children received partial merit scholarships upon admission to their colleges. So I consider earlier tuition payments an investment in their college costs.

My experience at my current school is that some students have their tuition paid by grandparents. What better gift could a child receive? And the grandparents could enjoy seeing the grandchild using their inheritance.

vate schools in 2000. That accounted for 24 percent of all schools in the U.S. and 10 percent of students.

But a private education doesn't come cheap. According to the National Association of Independent Schools, the median tuition for first grade at a private elementary school was $10,550 in 2001. The median tuition for 12th grade was $14,583. Of course, this varies according to region. Clearwater Central Catholic High School in Clearwater, Fla., charges $5,450 annually; the Chicago Waldorf School costs $10,400; a kid at Sidwell Friends School in Washington, D.C., will set you back $19,990.

FINANCIAL AID

Any money the school provides will come from its own coffers or private benefactors. Thus, the amount of aid a private elementary and secondary school can provide is limited. Your best bet is to endear yourself to those in charge of such matters at the school. They will tell you how to apply for aid and point out any scholarship programs available in your area.

Most schools aspire to a diverse student body, so numerous factors are considered when financial aid is disbursed. If there is any way your student stands out— any attributes or talents that would make him more attractive—make those known, too. Also, make sure the school is aware of any special financial circumstances, such as having to support elderly parents, extraordinary medical expenses, or a recent loss of income.

OTHER SOURCES OF AID

If you've already bugged the folks at your school enough, here are other avenues to explore:

- If the school is part of a larger system (e.g., a diocese), contact its headquarters. Many have their own departments of tuition assistance.

- The National Association of Independent Schools (NAIS) boasts a membership of 1,100 private schools from around the country. It provides general information about paying for a private education, as well as a list of scholarship providers, at www.nais.org. Some of these scholarships are open to everyone, but mostly only to students of a particular age, religion, ethnicity, or region.

- Many employers offer scholarships, usually intended to pay for college. Ask the benefits department at your place of employment whether the money also applies to other levels of education.

- Private scholarships are not well advertised, so you'll have to do some digging. Since most private aid is local, you'll have more luck scouring your own backyard.

- If you are a member of a particular ethnic, religious, professional, recreational, or fraternal group, contact the headquarters or local chapter of related associations and inquire about education assistance. Most of these funds are earmarked for college scholarships, but perhaps your powers of persuasion can open some minds, and coffers.

- Though uncommon, some schools publish financial aid information on their websites. It might be worthwhile to visit some websites to get leads on other sources of aid. Start with the schools in your area.

- School vouchers are available in some parts of the country, most prominently in Florida, Cleveland, and Milwaukee. Even if you live in one of the few school systems with a voucher program, participation might depend on your income or the status of your local public school. Visit SchoolChoiceInfo.org to see if you are eligible for tuition assistance. The site also lists a few private providers of scholarships.

OLD-FASHIONED SAVING

If you start early enough, you can stash away money now so the tuition bill won't hurt so much later. With other goals to save for—such as retirement and college—this takes some careful arrangement of priorities. However, if you do decide to set a little aside, or you suddenly come into some money, there are a couple of tax-friendly places to put the money until you need it.

The first is the Coverdell Education Savings Account. Formerly known as the Education IRA, and originally only used for college expenses, the money in a Coverdell ESA can now be used for tuition, room and board, uniforms, computers, school supplies, and other qualified expenses associated with a private education.

The money in a Coverdell ESA grows tax-free as long as it is eventually used for qualified expenses. Since taxes can consume anywhere from 10 to 45 percent of your earnings, this is significant. We discuss the Coverdell ESA in much greater detail in Chapter 3.

Besides the Coverdell, there are a couple of other noteworthy accounts, affectionately known as UGMA and UTMA. Besides sounding like the names of cave-dwelling twins, these accounts (which take their names from the Uniform Gift to Minors Act and the Uniform Transfer to Minors Act) are ways to give children money and realize some tax savings. Whether you open an UGMA or UTMA is contingent upon which state you reside, but they're similar. You, as the custodian, would control the money until the beneficiary reaches the age of majority (anywhere from 18 to 25, depending on the state).

The first $750 in earnings in an UGMA or UTMA are tax-free, the next $750 are taxed at 10 percent, and all earnings thereafter are taxed at the parents' tax bracket. So it's not as sweet as the completely tax-free treatment of earnings in a Coverdell ESA, which is why you should consider maxing out a Coverdell first before putting money in an UGMA or UTMA. The pros and cons of cus-

ODDS AND ENDS

Looking for other ways to pare the pain of parochial pedagogy? Here are some ideas:

- **Pay in installments:** Most schools allow you to pay tuition through no-interest monthly payments instead of one or two lump sums. There usually is an enrollment fee for the service, but it may be a small price to pay for not having to come up with the annual tuition all at once.

- **Explore the barter system:** Is there a service you could provide the school in exchange for lower tuition? Can you do some bookkeeping, maintenance, landscaping, or administrative work? Are you experienced in hypnotizing hundreds of kids into behaving during school assemblies? Most schools don't make this type of exchange official policy, but it wouldn't hurt to suggest some tit for tat. Also, most schools give breaks to employees, so find out if there is an opening you'd be qualified to fill.

- **Look for hand-me-downs:** If your school requires students to wear uniforms, consider buying ones others have outgrown. Some schools have established programs that facilitate uniform exchanges.

- **Does your school Scrip?** Scrip is a program that allows a coupon or card to be used instead of money to buy goods and services from participating retailers. The school buys Scrip at a discount, sells it at full price, and pockets the difference. For example, Mater Dei High School in Santa Ana, Calif., gives parents a 3 percent tuition rebate on Scrip purchases. Though Development Director Sue Harrison concedes that it can take a lot of Scrip to make a dent, every little bit helps.

continued...

...continued

- **Buy used books online:** If books are not included in the tuition, you can save a lot by purchasing books from other students or shopping at online used-book stores, such as Half.com, eCampus.com, the Amazon.com marketplace, and others.

todial accounts are discussed in Chapter 9. (We bet you can't wait.)

Note that the value of a Coverdell or a custodial account will affect financial aid eligibility when it's time to apply for college. Since funds in these accounts are considered the student's assets, they will reduce the amount of aid offered more than if the assets were owned by the parents. The differences between student and parental assets are discussed in breathless detail in Chapter 7.

GET BUSY: PAYING FOR A PRIVATE ELEMENTARY OR SECONDARY EDUCATION

Covering the costs of tuition is a many-splintered thing; it'll take exploring several avenues and testing a few strategies:

Step 1: Start saving

If you have a year (or a few) to save up, start socking away a little bit each month in a Coverdell ESA or custodial account.

Step 2: Apply to the school, and ask about financial aid

Be mindful of deadlines, and apply as soon as possible. Deadlines fall between December and May of the year before enrollment, most of them before the April 15 tax deadline. If receiving a generous aid package will dictate whether your child goes to a private school, apply to more than one school to increase your chances of getting enough assistance.

Step 3: Explore other aid possibilities

Scour the Internet and query organizations for benefactors. Tuition assistance for a private elementary or secondary education is out there, but it won't come looking for you.

Step 4: Ask about payment plans

Many schools have contracted with third-party companies that allow parents to pay tuition in interest-free installments, instead of in one, bulbous, hairy lump sum. If participation in such an arrangement *does* entail paying interest, then what you have is a loan—and probably a bad idea. Unless it's a one-time event, borrowing money to pay for a private pre-college education may be too much of a strain on the family finances.

ive
ast
acts

1. Get ready for sticker shock. Tuition and room and board can run from $10,000 to $35,000 annually. And since tuition increases have historically outpaced overall inflation, expect to see *much* bigger price tags in the future.

2. Don't despair. A lot of help awaits you, especially in the form of the $90 billion in financial aid distributed annually.

3. Perhaps the most significant factor in how much college will cost is the type of institution a student attends: an in-state public school, an out-of-state public school, or a private school. A higher tuition does not necessarily buy a better education.

4. Through the miracle of modern math, you can estimate how much college might cost when your child enrolls, and how much you need to save now to cover those costs.

5. Whatever you do, just start saving *something*. Saving $100 a month for 18 years could create a college savings account worth almost $50,000 (assuming an 8 percent annual return).

Chapter 2

Paying for College— An Overview

In this chapter...
- The rising costs of college
- Public vs. private schools
- How much you should save
- Do something now!

You're not going to like what you're about to read, but you probably suspect as much. You most likely have a sense of looming unpleasantness, the kind of feeling you get right before you open a container of leftovers that's been in the fridge for a year or two. But it's time to face reality. So let's just get this out of the way:

A COLLEGE EDUCATION CAN BE VERY, VERY EXPENSIVE!

Here's the naked-as-what's-beneath-a-toga truth: According to the College Board, an association of more than 4,200 U.S. schools that is best known for administering the Scholastic Aptitude Test (SAT), the average college tuition costs for the 2002-2003 school year were $4,081 for a public four-year college and $18,273 for a private four-year college. Those price tags are up 9.6 and 5.8 percent, respectively, from the previous year, which demonstrates an enduring aspect of college costs: They rise faster than overall inflation.

Add room and board and those annual average costs jump to $9,663 for a public school and $25,052 for a private school. That's just for one year, folks. By the time Junior earns a degree, the total will be more than four times those amounts (or seven times, depending on how often your little prince changes majors).

But don't despair! There is good news. Consider these stats from the same school year (also from the College Board):

- Almost 40 percent of students attending a four-year college paid less than $4,000 in tuition and fees.

- Almost 70 percent of students attending a four-year college paid less than $8,000 in tuition and fees.

- Only 7 percent of students attended schools that charge $24,000 or more for tuition.

Embedded in those numbers is an important lesson: There's a big difference between the "average" price tag of a college education and what most people actually pay. You can do a lot to keep college costs under control, from choosing a reasonably priced school to grabbing a piece of the $90 billion financial aid pie.

PUBLIC VS. PRIVATE

One of the biggest determinants of how much college will cost is whether your student chooses to attend your state's public university, another state's school, or a private college. Turn to page 14 for a sample of some tuition and room and board costs for an undergraduate.

Is a Tulane education worth more than 10 times a University of Florida education? It's a hotly debated topic, so you'll have to make your own call.

In 2000, the National Bureau of Economic Research published a paper in which the earnings of graduates of "elite" schools (as measured by average SAT scores of their graduates) were compared to the income of those accepted to these schools but then chose to go elsewhere. The study found that graduates of more selective schools did not earn more than those from less prestigious ones. In fact, it discovered that a greater indication of future earnings is the school to which a student applied, whether he was accepted or not. According to Princeton University economist Alan Krueger, who co-authored the study, "It appears that student ambition, as reflected in the quality of the school to which he or she applies, is a better predictor of earning success than what college they ultimately choose or which college chooses them." The study calls this the "Steven

PUBLIC INSTITUTIONS

School	Tuition	Room & Board
University of Florida	$2,630 ($12,096 nonresidents)	$5,470
Arizona State University	$2,508 ($8,520 nonresidents)	$5,866
University of Nebraska	$4,167 ($10,760 nonresidents)	$4,875
University of California (Berkeley)	$4,200 ($11,502 nonresidents)	$9,747
University of Maryland	$5,341 ($13,413 nonresidents)	$6,784
University of Michigan	$7,485 ($23,365 nonresidents)	$6,372

PRIVATE INSTITUTIONS

School	Tuition	Room & Board
Rice University	$16,660	$7,200
St. Olaf College	$22,200	$4,750
Yale University	$27,130	$8,240
Stanford University	$27,204	$8,680
Princeton University	$27,230	$7,842
Reed College	$27,360	$7,380
Tulane University	$28,310	$7,392

Spielberg Effect" because the filmmaker, though rejected by two of the most prestigious film schools in the country, has been immensely successful at making movies about bloodthirsty sharks, dinosaurs, and Nazis (*E.T. The Extra-Terrestrial* excluded).

So the secret to your kid's future financial success is to make sure he applies to Harvard, even if he's... well...

a few pins short of a strike when it comes to academic ability.

OK, not really. But keep these in mind as you wrangle with the "public vs. private" issue:

- Private colleges know that they're much more expensive, and thus are prepared to offer more aid. Don't write off a big-ticket school for financial reasons. You could end up with an aid package from a private school that makes attendance cheaper than going to an in-state public university.

- If your student knows what she wants to study, then look for schools that excel in that field. Not every department at a prestigious school is necessarily held in the highest esteem, and some of the best programs in the country are offered by public schools. For example, four of the top five undergraduate marketing programs (as ranked by *U.S. News & World Report*) are offered by public institutions.

- A college education is generally one of the few investments worth borrowing money for. But that doesn't mean it's OK to take out loans willy-nilly. If you, or the student, will end up with a degree *and* a burdensome IOU, question whether the pricier school is worth it.

For more wisdom and perspective, listen to what these Fool readers had to say about whether costly schools were worth the price of admission:

> *I'm quite sure I'll never recover (financially) the difference between my MIT education and the one that I could have gotten from my local state school, but I don't regret it for a moment. My immersion in that environment is a large part of who I am today, 15 years later. I consider the investment worthwhile; life is a one-shot deal and regrets are often more expensive than financial liabilities.* —Mike

> *If you (or your kid) know what you want to study—say, nursing or teaching—after graduation your salaries will be the same, regardless of whether you got your teaching degree from Harvard or from your local public college. There are many jobs in the public or not-for-profit sector where your salary is negotiated by your union, and you'll all start out pretty much the same.* —Christiane

> *College is more than just a means of entry into financial markets. Ideally, an undergraduate education gives you a sense of history, makes you write a lot,*

*insists you give reasons for your opin-
ions, shows you how science works,
makes you realize that we are not the
only country in the world, etc. This is
what once was called 'education for cit-
izenship' and I have no idea how you
can put a valuation on it. I still think it
is a far more appropriate goal for a university than just educating people to go
into a workforce.* —*Patrick*

*I graduated from Tufts University in
Medford, Mass., which at the time was
the eighth most expensive school in the
United States. Luckily, I was poor—my
single-parent mom went to college the
same year. So between scholarships,
grants, loans, and working during the
school year and all vacations, it worked
out to be cheaper than the University of
New Hampshire [my in-state option].
I believe the fact that I was smart, fe-
male, and poor helped a great deal. But,
boy, am I happy that I didn't have to
spend all that money to get my degree.*
—*Terri*

HOW MUCH MIGHT IT COST?

Given such variables as inflation and the wide-ranging
prices charged by schools, how much should you plan

GO, BANANA SLUGS!

When you attend an institution of higher learning, it becomes part of your identity. Once you've attended Notre Dame, you become one of the Fighting Irish. If you graduate from Indiana University, you'll forever be a Hoosier. So before enrolling, make sure you're comfortable with a school's mascot, especially any of these:

- The Chokers (Grays Hill Community College)

- The Anteaters (U. of California at Irvine)

- The Fightin' Mules (Central Missouri State)

- The Artichokes (Scottsdale Community College)

- The Icabods (Washburn University)

- The Sycamores (Indiana State)

- The Gamecocks (University of South Carolina)

- The Ducks (University of Oregon)

- The Beavers (Oregon State)

- The Fighting Okra (Delta State University)

- The Banana Slugs (U. of California at Santa Cruz)

to have ready by the time your pride and joy goes to college? Here are some ideas:

1. **Plan to pay for an in-state public education:** For the 2002-2003 school year, 54 percent of full-time students were enrolled in schools that charged $4,999 or less in tuition and fees. And that doesn't take into account any financial aid. Therefore, aiming to save enough to cover the costs of the average public education will put most people in good shape.

2. **Plan to pay about $8,000 (in 2002 prices) per year:** Seventy percent of college students paid less than $8,000 a year for tuition, so it's a reasonable goal to shoot for, especially if you haven't settled the "public vs. private" dilemma.

3. **Plan to pay the full private tuition and room and board:** If your child is destined for a private school, and you don't anticipate receiving financial aid, then plan to pay about $100,000 (at 2002 prices) for a four-year degree.

GETTING SPECIFIC

You can approximate the cost of a post-secondary education and how much you need to save per month to have that money when you need it. Here are two tables that project the annual costs of attending college. One table projects just the increases in tuition, the other tuition *and* room and board, using the average tuition

COLLEGE COSTS: TUITION ONLY

Year	In-State Public University	Reasonable Target	Private University
2002	4,081	8,000	18,273
2003	4,326	8,480	19,369
2004	4,585	8,989	20,532
2005	4,861	9,528	21,763
2006	5,152	10,100	23,069
2007	5,461	10,706	24,453
2008	5,789	11,348	25,921
2009	6,136	12,029	27,476
2010	6,504	12,751	29,124
2011	6,895	13,516	30,872
2012	7,308	14,327	32,724
2013	7,747	15,186	34,688
2014	8,212	16,098	36,769
2015	8,704	17,063	38,975
2016	9,227	18,087	41,313
2017	9,780	19,172	43,792
2018	10,367	20,323	46,420
2019	10,989	21,542	49,205
2020	11,649	22,835	52,157
2021	12,347	24,205	55,287
2022	13,088	25,657	58,604
2023	13,874	27,197	62,120
2024	14,706	28,828	65,847
2025	15,588	30,558	69,798
2026	16,524	32,391	73,986
2027	17,515	34,335	78,425
2028	18,566	36,395	83,131
2029	19,680	38,579	88,119
2030	20,861	40,893	93,406

COLLEGE COSTS: TUITION, ROOM AND BOARD

Year	In-State Public University	Reasonable Target	Private University
2002	9,663	14,000	25,052
2003	10,243	14,840	26,555
2004	10,857	15,730	28,148
2005	11,509	16,674	29,837
2006	12,199	17,675	31,628
2007	12,931	18,735	33,525
2008	13,707	19,859	35,537
2009	14,530	21,051	37,669
2010	15,401	22,314	39,929
2011	16,325	23,653	42,325
2012	17,305	25,072	44,864
2013	18,343	26,576	47,556
2014	19,444	28,171	50,410
2015	20,610	29,861	53,434
2016	21,847	31,653	56,640
2017	23,158	33,552	60,039
2018	24,547	35,565	63,641
2019	26,020	37,699	67,459
2020	27,581	39,961	71,507
2021	29,236	42,358	75,797
2022	30,991	44,900	80,345
2023	32,850	47,594	85,166
2024	34,821	50,450	90,276
2025	36,910	53,476	95,692
2026	39,125	56,685	101,434
2027	41,472	60,086	107,520
2028	43,961	63,691	113,971
2029	46,598	67,513	120,809
2030	49,394	71,564	128,058

costs for the 2002-2003 school year. If you haven't answered the "public vs. private" question, then consider the middle "reasonable target" column (based on $8,000 for tuition and $6,000 for room and board). From there, we assumed a 6 percent rate of inflation for higher-education costs.

Here's how to estimate your future college expenses and a monthly savings target:

1. Add up the costs for the four years your child will be in college.

2. Multiply that number by a return factor from the following table. The return factor can be found at the intersection of the number of years until your child enrolls and the return you expect to earn on your savings. (If you don't know what rate of return to use, try somewhere between 4 and 8 percent, depending on how conservative or aggressive you are with your investments.)

3. The result is the amount you should save each month to meet your goal.

4. Fall on the floor.

If you'd like to confirm your calculations, or you'd rather have a computer do the math, fiddle with the "What will it take to save for a college education?" calculator at www.Fool.com/calcs/calculators.htm.

COLLEGE SAVINGS RETURN FACTORS

% Return	1 Year	3 Years	5 Years	10 Years	15 Years	20 Years
2%	0.07616	0.02622	0.01559	0.00474	0.00338	0.00338
3%	0.07578	0.02583	0.01520	0.00709	0.00438	0.00303
4%	0.07540	0.02544	0.01481	0.00672	0.00403	0.00271
5%	0.07502	0.02505	0.01443	0.00637	0.00371	0.00242
6%	0.07464	0.02467	0.01406	0.00604	0.00341	0.00215
7%	0.07427	0.02429	0.01370	0.00571	0.00313	0.00190
8%	0.07389	0.02392	0.01334	0.00540	0.00286	0.00168
9%	0.07352	0.02355	0.01299	0.00510	0.00262	0.00148
10%	0.07315	0.02319	0.01265	0.00482	0.00239	0.00130

DON'T GET SCARED OUT OF SAVING

Some people, when they see such astronomical price tags attached to a college degree, do something extraordinary: They do nothing. They figure there's no way to save that much without shortchanging other goals, so they cross their fingers and hope their little Einstein will win large scholarships or join an anti-education cult.

Don't fall for this trap. If you start soon enough, you can have a large chunk of higher-education money when your progeny is ready to enroll in P.U. If as soon as their kid is born, a couple invests $100 a month and earns 8 percent per year, they'd have almost $50,000 in 18 years (assuming they use a tax-friendly savings vehicle, which we'll discuss presently). That's $50,000 less that you or your kid will have to borrow.

Even if your offspring is in high school and you haven't saved a dime, don't give up. Whatever you do... do whatever you can. Really, every little bit helps.

Where should you put those monthly savings? We're glad you asked. There are three main places to put your college savings: the Coverdell Education Savings Account, a 529 prepaid tuition plan, or a 529 savings plan. Want to know the details? Then turn to the next chapter.

THE MORE I SAVE, THE LESS FINANCIAL AID I'LL GET, SO WHY BOTHER?

The amount of money you have saved for school will likely reduce the size of your financial aid package. However, don't let that deter you from saving. Here's why:

- Most financial aid comes in the form of loans. The less you save now, the more you may have to borrow—and pay back, with interest—later.

- There's no guarantee that you'll be eligible for much aid even if you don't save.

- Some types of accounts are more financial aid-friendly than others. Money in the parents' name, for example, will have a much gentler impact on financial aid eligibility than money in the student's name.

Five Fast Facts

1. Earnings in a Coverdell Education Savings Account grow tax-free as long as the money is used for qualified elementary, secondary, or post-secondary education expenses.

2. The annual contribution limit for a Coverdell is $2,000 per student. If you plan to contribute more than two grand a year, look into a 529 plan. However, this is not an "either/or" situation. A student can be the beneficiary of both a Coverdell and a 529 plan.

3. The assets in a Coverdell are considered the student's property, which will have a big effect on financial aid (as compared to assets owned by the parents). Keep in mind, though, that the money in a Coverdell can be transferred to a 529 plan, where assets do not belong to the student and thus have a less harmful impact on financial aid.

4. If you desire maximum control over your investments—in terms of what you can buy, and how often you transact—this is the education savings account for you.

5. As with all investment accounts, keep fees to a minimum.

The Coverdell ESA

In 1997, the Education IRA was born. It was a puny, puzzling thing, because the annual contribution limit was just $500—and what did saving for education have to do with an individual retirement account? But laws enacted in 2001 changed all that. The annual contribution limit was quadrupled to $2,000, and the Education IRA was renamed the Coverdell Education Savings Account, in honor of the late Senator Paul Coverdell of Georgia.

The earnings in the account grow tax-free as long as distributions are used for eligible expenses, which are not limited to college costs. Coverdell funds can also be used to cover costs associated with attending elementary or secondary school, be it public, private, or religious. These costs can include uniforms, tutoring, computers, and transportation. (Sorry, juice boxes and horse camp don't count.)

A "responsible individual" controls the account and chooses the investments, which can be stocks, bonds, mutual funds, or cash equivalents. (Note: Even though you can never find your car keys, and you occasionally put shirts in the baby seat and drop your kids off at the cleaners, there is only one test you must pass to be the "responsible individual": Are you the parent or legal guardian of the child? If so, you can control the account. Grandparents, rich aunts, and benevolent dictators—no matter how consistently they floss and eat their vegetables—cannot be the responsible individual on another child's account, even if they make contributions.)

Any individual may contribute to a Coverdell ESA for the benefit of anyone under age 18. But the contribution limit is reduced for those with a modified adjusted gross income between $95,000 and $110,000 for single persons and between $190,000 and $220,000 for joint filers. The amount of the reduction depends on your income. For example, if you're single and earn halfway between $95,000 and $110,000, then you can contribute $1,000— half of the maximum. If you're single and you earn $110,001, then you're out of luck.

But even if you exceed those income limits, don't worry. Give the money to the kid and let him open the Coverdell ESA himself. For example, let's say Jocelyn, a single person, wants to establish a Coverdell ESA for her favorite little guy, Lukas. But Jocelyn's AGI is $130,000. Her maximum contribution to little Lukas' Coverdell ESA would be zero, zip, zilch—because of the income limitation rules. But there is no reason that Jocelyn can't make a $2,000 gift to Lukas, who then opens his own Coverdell ESA, since he's well under the income limitations (assuming his lemonade stand doesn't rake in more than $95,000 a year).

While the $2,000 limit is considerably less than that placed on 529 plans, you can still accumulate a tidy sum if you start early enough. If you begin maxing out a Coverdell when your child is born, the account could be worth approximately $80,000 by high school graduation (assuming 8 percent annual growth).

You have until the due date of your tax return (not including extensions) to contribute and still have it apply to the previous year.

Contributions can no longer be made once the beneficiary turns 18 years old, and funds must be used by the time he's 30. However, the account can be transferred to a relative (including cousins, step-relatives, and in-laws). If funds are used for a nonqualified expense, earnings will be assessed a 10 percent penalty and count as ordinary income to the beneficiary.

THE FINANCIAL AID FACTOR

Money in a Coverdell ESA is counted among the student's assets (as opposed to the parents'). When it comes to calculating need, the standard financial aid formula factors in a larger portion of the student's assets. Therefore, money in a Coverdell ESA can reduce the student's chances of being awarded need-based financial aid.

In terms of financial aid, this makes a Coverdell ESA less appealing than a 529 savings plan. Distributions from a Coverdell are treated as the student's income for the following year. Students are expected to contribute 50 percent of their income toward school, so withdrawals will reduce eligibility for the following year. (See Chapter 7: Financial Aid for more information.)

Since policies that regulate the financial aid process change *all the time*, you need to stay abreast of the shifting landscape and act quickly. The Coverdell ESA is still in its formative years, so there's no telling how the financial aid formulas will treat it as it ages.

GET BUSY: CHOOSING AND OPENING A COVERDELL EDUCATION SAVINGS ACCOUNT

If you've ever opened a brokerage or mutual fund account, then opening a Coverdell will be a snap. If you haven't, then it'll just be a few snaps.

Step 1: Find the right account

Coverdell ESAs, like any other investment account, are offered by brokerage firms, mutual fund companies, and banks (but not all, so you'll have to ask around). As with any investment account, you should keep these tips in mind as you shop:

- **Keep fees and commissions low:** A $30 annual fee added to a $20 commission will eat 2.5 percent of your $2,000 contribution (and even more if you contribute less). In particular, watch out for "inactivity fees," which is how brokerages punish you for not generating enough commissions.

- **Make sure you get the right choice of investments:** Does the account offer the range of investments you're interested in?

- **Look for the right features:** Determine which attributes—such as phone trades, research products, or local offices—are important to you.

If you don't have an account provider in mind, start with the low-cost leaders. For mutual funds, check out Vanguard, T. Rowe Price, and TIAA-CREF. If you want to be able to purchase individual stocks, bonds, or other investments, set up a discount brokerage account.

As you shop around, use the chart on the next page to keep track of who offers (and charges) what.

Step 2: Open and fund the account
Most enrollment forms are available on the Internet. You can choose to send in your contribution to the account

COVERDELL EDUCATION SAVINGS ACCOUNT COMPARISON CHART			
Provider			
Annual Account Fees			
Commissions and Other Charges			
Investment Options			
Other Features			

in one lump sum, or bit by bit. One of the easiest ways to invest is through an automatic transfer program. Money is sent directly from your bank account to your Coverdell ESA; the amount and frequency is up to you. For example, if you want to contribute the maximum amount each year ($2,000), transfer $166 to the Coverdell each month. This method of investing is best used with mutual funds, since buying individual stocks or bonds in such small increments is cost-prohibitive.

Step 3: Choose your investment(s)

We discuss investing for school in Chapter 10, but—as we just indicated—it can be prohibitively expensive to invest small amounts of money in individual stocks and bonds. As a Foolish rule of thumb, commissions should not consume more than 2 percent of your principal. If you contribute $2,000 to a Coverdell account that charges a $20 commission per trade, then you should put that money in no more than two investments. Is that enough diversification? Perhaps not—which is why mutual funds with an expense ratio of less than 1 percent might be a better investment until your account is worth several thousand dollars.

Five Fast Facts

1. A prepaid tuition plan allows contributors to purchase tomorrow's tuition at today's prices, or at a slight premium to current prices. Disbursements from prepaid plans are tax-free when used for qualified expenses. Otherwise, taxes and a 10 percent penalty will be assessed.

2. State-sponsored prepaid tuition plans typically are open only to contributors or beneficiaries who are residents. A consortium of private colleges, called Tuition Plan, will begin offering its own prepaid plan in July 2003.

3. If you don't attend a school that participates in your prepaid plan, your investment can be used at another school, but there's no guarantee that the value of your account will cover tuition entirely.

4. Prepaid tuition plans are most attractive to investors who like the peace of mind that comes from knowing a certain amount of tuition will be covered, regardless of tuition inflation and stock-market gyration.

5. Enrollment typically is not open all year, and usually not available to high school students beyond the freshman or sophomore year.

Chapter 4

The 529 Prepaid Tuition Plan

In this chapter...
- Buying tomorrow's tuition today
- Effect on financial aid
- Opening a 529 prepaid tuition plan

First conceived on a wintry night (wink, wink) in the 1980s, prepaid tuition plans became part of Section 529 of the Internal Revenue Code in 1996. Essentially, these programs allow participants to buy tomorrow's tuition at today's prices, or at a little bit more than today's prices. Thus, regardless of future tuition increases, the number of quarters/semesters/years purchased today are guaranteed for the future—but only if the student attends a school covered by the plan. She must attend an in-state public institution to get the guarantee of a state-sponsored plan.

Note: We're using the term "guaranteed" loosely here. Not all of these plans are backed by the full faith and credit of the sponsor state, and the bear market that started in 2000 has put a strain on some of these programs. Find out exactly what guarantees you have with your plan. Also, enrollment in a prepaid plan does not influence a student's acceptance at participating schools.

There are two forms of prepaid plans. The most common, called the *contract* plan, goes thusly: The state says, "You pay a lump sum of $____ right now, or $____ each month for the next ____ years, and tuition will be covered for any public institution of higher education in this state."

The *credit* plan, on the other hand, converts money you contribute into credit. When it's time for your student to go to college, your total number of credits will buy a certain amount of tuition, and perhaps room and board. For example, units in Ohio's Guaranteed Savings Plan cost 1 percent of the average tuition at each of the state's 13 four-year colleges. Then, a premium is added to "ensure actuarial soundness" (i.e., make sure the plan doesn't go broke). As of October 1, 2002, the price of a unit in Ohio's plan was $80. If the student goes to one of its public colleges in the future, each unit will cover 1 percent of the then-current tuition.

Because it's difficult to anticipate where a student will go to college, most states have provisions for using the savings in the plan to pay for tuition at a private or out-of-state school. However, states will not guarantee that your account will cover tuition at another school. Your contract will be valued based on the state's tuition rates, or you'll just get back your contributions, usually with some interest.

Some prepaid plans cover only tuition and fees; other plans will also pay for room and board. If you participate in a plan that does not cover room and board, you'll have to save separately for those expenses. A prepaid tuition plan can be transferred to another family member.

Public colleges aren't the only schools that offer prepaid plans. Beginning on July 1, 2003, a consortium of almost 300 private schools will offer a prepaid tuition plan, known as... Tuition Plan. The plan does not charge enrollment or maintenance fees, and each school will also add a tuition rate discount as part of the deal. You do not have to choose a school when you enroll. President and CEO Doug Brown likens the plan to buying a gift certificate for an entire mall: Once it's time to cash in, you have a range of places to spend your money, but your money will go farther at some places than others. Visit www.tuition plan.org or call (877) 874-0740 for more information.

THE FINANCIAL AID FACTOR

Of the three major types of college savings accounts, the prepaid tuition plan has the most harmful effect on need-based financial aid. The assets in the plan reduce a student's need dollar for dollar. If your family is in the middle to lower income bracket, which increases your chance for need-based aid, then you should consider carefully whether you want to enroll in a prepaid plan and risk missing out on scholarships or grants.

However, there is a movement afoot to have all this changed. In fact, some states are recharacterizing their plans as "guaranteed savings" plans in hopes of securing kinder treatment from financial aid formulas. This is a development worth monitoring.

GET BUSY: CHOOSING AND OPENING A PREPAID TUITION PLAN

No matter where you live in America, a stock is a stock, a mutual fund is a mutual fund, and an IRA is an IRA. Not so with tuition plans. Each prepaid tuition plan has its own rules and regulations. Here's help on how to make an informed decision:

Step 1: Find out if your state offers a prepaid tuition plan

Poke around the websites of your state's colleges, treasurer's office, or visit SavingforCollege.com—the definitive source for all things 529. Most plans are only open to benefactors or beneficiaries who are residents. If your state does not provide a plan, then your only other option might be the Tuition Plan mentioned earlier.

Step 2: Learn the nitty-gritty about the plan

Before you sign up, get answers to these questions:

- **Is the tuition benefit guaranteed?** Find out what would happen if the money in the plan's trust fund isn't enough to pay for all participants' benefits.

- **Is a premium added to today's tuition prices?** A certain amount of money might be added to the current price of tuition in determining the price of a unit. The bigger the premium, the lower the "return" on your investment.

- **What will happen if I don't attend a participating school?** Will you get back just your contributions, or will the plan determine a value of your account that includes some interest?

- **When can I sign up?** Most prepaid plans do not have year-round enrollment, and many are not available to students beyond the freshman or sophomore years of high school.

- **Can I deduct contributions on my state income tax return?** If so, how much—the entire contribution, or just a portion?

Step 3: Sign up

If you're convinced a prepaid plan is for you, download the enrollment forms from the Internet. Plans allow for either a lump-sum investment or an installment plan. Installment payments can be made by automatic transfer (some plans even offer incentives to do so), and possibly through payroll deduction.

Five Fast Facts

1. The 529 savings plan offers a triumvirate of benefits: tax-free growth, high contribution limits, and no income limits.

2. You don't have to enroll in your state's plan, so look for one with low expenses and attractive investment options. Plans vary significantly from state to state, so do your homework.

3. Though you can join another state's plan, yours might offer incentives, such as a deduction on your state income tax return. Also, while savings generally reduce financial aid eligibility, some states ignore assets in its own 529 plan when doling out aid to students who attend an in-state public or private school.

4. You can't manage your investments directly. You must choose from among the plan's mutual fund-type investments. You can change investments, or transfer to another 529 plan, once every 12 months.

5. Money in a 529 plan is considered the property of the contributor, not the beneficiary, which lessens the impact on financial aid eligibility. However, the withdrawals might be considered the student's income for the following year, which is not so financial aid-friendly. If this is the case, allocate 529 savings to the latter years of college.

The 529 College Savings Plan

In that fine American tradition of conferring boring names on exciting government creations (e.g., the White House, the Pentagon, 401(k), 403(b), Area 51, Bigfoot, the grassy knoll), Uncle Sam invented an outstanding college savings account and named it after a tax code: Section 529.

A 529 savings plan is, in essence, an investment account. Unlike a 529 prepaid tuition plan, it does not lock in future tuition costs. Instead, it is an opportunity for investments to grow through the years at rates that equal—or better yet, exceed—increases in college costs.

Investments grow federally tax-free as long as the money is used to pay for qualified higher-education expenses (tuition, fees, books, supplies, and room and board). While contributions are not deductible on your federal tax return, some states permit a partial or complete state tax deduction to residents who participate in the state's plan.

The tax-free status of withdrawals will continue until 2011, when the current law "sunsets." At that point, withdrawals will be considered the student's income—unless Congress votes to make permanent this tax-free status, which most experts anticipate it will (a bill has been introduced in the House).

Anyone may contribute to a 529 plan. You don't even have to live in the state of the plan that you choose. You could live in one state and contribute to a plan sponsored by another state for your grandchild who lives in a third state and goes to college in a fourth state. If you think you might go back to school someday, most plans will even allow you to set up an account for yourself.

In most cases, you can contribute more than $200,000 over the life of your account. Most plans have no age or income limitations, so higher-bracket taxpayers can also participate. Unlike in a custodial account (e.g., UGMA and UTMA), you retain control of assets in a 529 plan. With only a few exceptions, your kids can't grab the money and run off to Europe when they reach the age of majority. You decide when distributions are made, and for what the funds will be used. (At last, something you can lord over the kids after they turn 18!)

If you remove the earnings from your account without spending them on higher-education expenses, you'll pay taxes and get zapped with a 10 percent penalty. However, most plans will allow you to change beneficiaries. So, if your child decides not to attend college, you can transfer the account to someone directly related to your kid (including cousins, step-relatives, and in-laws).

Perhaps the biggest knock on 529 savings plans is their inflexibility. You can't directly manage the funds yourself; you must choose a money manager (think mutual fund). The number of investment options varies from plan to plan, ranging from only a few funds to almost 30. Also, once you've chosen your asset allocation, you can't change the mix for 12 months. If you're not happy with the plan itself, you can transfer to another—but just once every 12 months.

THE FINANCIAL AID FACTOR

Assets in a 529 savings plan are considered the property of the contributor, not the beneficiary. This is pretty peachy when it comes to financial aid eligibility, since students are expected to contribute a larger portion of their assets and income than their parents.

There is one caveat: Though the assets don't belong to the student, withdrawals might count as income for the following year, and students are expected to contribute

ESTATE PLANNING, ANYONE?

There's a neat estate-planning aspect to 529 plans that can reduce a taxable estate much quicker than the current $11,000 annual gift exclusion. You can contribute in one year the maximum limit to a 529 plan and treat it as if it were a gift made over a five-year period. In other words, you could at once fund your child's 529 plan with $55,000 ($110,000 for couples) tax-free, since that amount would be considered as $11,000 ($22,000 for couples) annually made over a five-year period.

50 percent of their income toward school. Since 529 plans are so new, a definite, standard treatment of withdrawals hasn't yet been established. Do some research before you make any decisions, and if you're worried about how taking withdrawals from a 529 plan will affect financial aid, then allocate your 529 savings to the junior and senior years of college.

GET BUSY: CHOOSING AND ENROLLING IN A 529 SAVINGS PLAN

Just a few years ago, if you said "529," most people would have thought of (what else?) the Edict of Emperor Justinian, which dissolved Plato's Academy in 529 A.D. But by now, most people have heard of 529 college savings plans, and every state has its own version. However, because the 529 universe is still developing, many plans have plenty of kinks to iron out. Here's how to choose the plan that's right for you:

Step 1: Start with your own state's plan

A good place to begin your search is SavingforCollege.com—the No. 1 source of information on 529 plans, rules, and regulations—and check out your state's plan, mostly to see if it offers perks to residents. Contributions to the state's 529 plan might be deductible on the state income tax return. Also, most states do not tax distributions from their own plans, but do not confer such munificent treatment on those from other states' plans. Also, when distributing aid, a state might ignore assets in its plan, thereby making applicants appear more "needy."

Step 2: Get the buzz about the best plans

Don't be tempted to go with your state's plan without comparison-shopping. Several financial publications—such as *Kiplinger's* and *Money* magazines—rank all the 529 plans. Make sure you review the latest analyses; the world of 529 plans is rapidly evolving.

Step 3: Evaluate several plans

Once you have the information on your state's plan, and an idea of which other plans are highly regarded, let the appraisals begin. To help you out, we've provided a spiffy chart, and, as an example, filled out the first column with information about Nebraska's 2002 savings plan (which *Money* magazine and *USA Today* voted as the best).

Here's what to look for in a 529 savings plan:

529 SAVINGS PLAN COMPARISON CHART				
Plan Name	College Savings Plan of Nebraska			
Residency Benefit	Nebraska residents can deduct contributions of up to $1,000 on the state income tax return. Nebraska state agencies must exclude money saved in the program when calculating financial aid eligibility for residents.			
Open to Non-residents?	Yes			
Annual Fees	$24 per year			
Commissions and Other Charges	0			
Expense Ratios on Funds	Less than 1% on all options			
Number of Investment Options	10			
Special Withdrawal Provisions	None			
Contribution Limit	$250,000 per lifetime of account			

BUY STUFF, SAVE FOR COLLEGE

How many times have you eaten a Big Mac and thought, "I'd feel better about clogging my arteries if only I were simultaneously contributing to my kid's college fund"?

We haven't, either. But now you can rationalize your fat intake by signing up for a college-savings rewards program, such as Upromise or BabyMint. Purchases from all kinds of retailers and service providers—such as Borders, Starbucks, America Online, Century 21, General Motors, and Verizon Wireless—can contribute money into a 529 plan.

By registering your credit card, or using a special credit card issued by an affiliate, your purchases are monitored for patronage of participating companies. (Yes, this raises privacy issues, which you should research and reconcile before signing up.) The rebates are automatically deposited to your college savings account. Your relatives can also enroll for your or your kids' benefit.

Used conscientiously, these programs can turn day-to-day spending into free tuition.

- **Low expenses:** Watch for enrollment fees, transfer fees, annual fees, and annual expenses on your investments. Don't consider plans with investments that charge much more than 1 percent a year. The lowest-cost plans often offer funds from Vanguard and TIAA-CREF.

- **No commission:** Some plans are only available through financial advisors, who don't work for free;

you may have to pay a commission of around 5 percent. That's only fair if you use the services of a pro. But if you're comfortable making your own investment decisions, then you'll save a lot of money with a commission-free plan.

- **A variety of good investments:** Some plans offer just a couple of ho-hum choices, whereas others present a menu of more than 20 mutual funds. More choices don't necessarily indicate a better plan, but you want options. Gauging performance can be difficult since most 529 savings plans have been around for only a few years (or less). The best you can do is to evaluate other funds managed by the same folks who are in charge of a 529's investments. Many plans proffer age-based portfolios, which automatically shift your money to more conservative investments as the student gets closer to high school graduation. (See Chapter 10: Investing for School for more information.)

- **Special withdrawal provisions:** Some programs have rules about how long assets can remain in the plan, or how long they must be in an account before they can be withdrawn. For example, you can't take money out of New York's plan for three years after opening the account.

- **Rides on the space shuttle:** If you find a plan that offers them, we recommend you seriously consider it. Unfortunately, no plan currently does.

Step 4: Sign up

Download the forms from the plan's website, fill in the blanks, and give the mailperson something to do. If you will be contributing in one fell swoop, include the check. Otherwise, sign up for the automatic investment option; having money electronically transferred from your bank account is convenient. Depending on the plan and your employer, contributions may also be deducted directly from your paycheck.

Which Is Best for You?

It's time to take the final for your college-savings course. Luckily for you, this is a multiple-choice test. To compare plan features side by side, review our handy-dandy College Savings Plans Comparison Chart at the end of this chapter.

If the financial aid treatment of savings in an account is a significant factor in your decision, make sure to get the most current information. Rules change constantly, so base your decision on up-to-date facts.

Now, let's get down to the basics.

WHY A PREPAID TUITION PLAN IS RIGHT FOR YOU:

- You're risk-averse.

- You like knowing your tuition will be covered.

- You're unsure you'll qualify for financial aid. Unlike the other options, assets in a prepaid tuition plan reduce financial aid eligibility dollar for dollar (though plan sponsors are lobbying for this to change).

WHY A PREPAID TUITION PLAN IS WRONG FOR YOU:

- A prepaid plan is not offered by your state or by the school your child wants to attend.

- You prefer to choose your own investments.

- Your children are young, so the longer time horizon will allow you to be more aggressive with your investments, potentially resulting in more money.

If you'd rather use an investment account to fund your or your child's college education, then you have another choice to make: Should you choose a Coverdell ESA or a 529 savings plan? Here are the most important considerations:

WHY A COVERDELL ESA IS PREFERABLE:

- Distributions are tax-free. So are distributions from a 529 plan—until 2011. Congress is likely to extend the tax-free treatment of distributions, but it's not a sure thing.

- You choose the investments. You can invest in stocks, bonds, mutual funds, or just plain old cash, and you can change the investments as often as you wish (but watch out for the commissions!). With a 529 plan, you must choose a money manager. On top of that, since most 529 plans are relatively new, these accounts have short histories, making it difficult to evaluate their quality.

- Funds in a Coverdell ESA can also be used for eligible elementary- and secondary-education expenses, as well as computers, tutors, and Internet access.

WHY A 529 SAVINGS PLAN IS PREFERABLE:

- Contribution limits to 529 plans are significantly higher.

- Assets in a Coverdell ESA are considered the student's property, which can reduce her financial aid package. On the other hand, assets in a 529 savings plan belong to the account owner.

- Your state may offer incentives for contributing to the local 529 plan. (Curious if your state does? The College Savings Plans Network has the answers at www.collegesavings.org/tax_treatment.htm.)

Keep in mind that you can transfer assets in a Coverdell to a 529 plan. So, if you like many aspects of the Coverdell, but are worried about its negative effect on your financial aid application, transfer the money before you apply.

THE GOOD NEWS

Thanks to the Economic Growth and Tax Relief Reconciliation Act of 2001, investors can simultaneously contribute to a Coverdell ESA and both types of 529s. Why would you do this? Here are a few scenarios:

- You want to diversify. You want some of your money to lock in a portion of future tuition costs through a prepaid plan, but you also want to see if your investing prowess can provide a better return.

- You've decided to enroll in a prepaid tuition plan, but you'd also like to save for room and board (which aren't covered by most prepaid tuition plans).

- You want to get the state tax deduction by investing in your state's program, but you don't want all your college savings in the hands of money managers, so you open a Coverdell ESA and make your own investment decisions.

- Your kids will go to college after 2010, and you don't want to risk Congress not extending the tax-free status of 529 withdrawals. So, you put the first

WHAT IF YOU'VE SAVED TOO MUCH?

You've scrimped and saved for years so you can cover the costs of a college education for your daughter—and she goes out and gets a full scholarship. (What an ingrate!) Or perhaps you saved more than necessary, or made some stellar investments. Whatever the reason, you have money left over in your college savings accounts.

Oh, to have such problems! And it is a problem: Taxes and penalties are assessed on withdrawals from 529 plans and Coverdell ESAs that are not used to cover qualified expenses. So what should you do with the leftovers? Ponder these possibilities:

- If the excess is due to the student receiving a merit- or need-based award, an amount equal to the award can be withdrawn without penalty, though taxes might be assessed.

- If the student might go back to school later, keep the account active (as long as the account doesn't have mandatory withdrawal limits—Coverdell funds, for example, can be used until the beneficiary turns 30).

- Coverdell and 529 accounts can be transferred to other family members (unless the money started out in an UGMA or UTMA).

- Withdraw the money, pay the taxes and penalties, and take a vacation—you deserve it! (Caveat: If you don't deserve it, send the money to people who do. You can find our mailing address at www.Fool.com.)

$2,000 in a Coverdell ESA, then put the rest in a 529 plan.

- You anticipate that your child will attend private elementary or secondary schools (or both), so you contribute to a Coverdell ESA. However, because contributions to a Coverdell ESA are limited to $2,000 a year, you are concerned that the funds in the account will not be enough to pay for elementary, secondary, *and* post-secondary school, so you also contribute to a 529 plan.

JUST DO SOMETHING!

Don't let all these deliberations prevent you from saving as soon as possible. Saving *something* is much better than delaying while you solve the college account conundrum. Due to the higher contribution limits and favorable financial aid treatment, 529 savings plans are good deals for most people. If your state offers benefits for participating in its 529 plan, and the plan includes at least five investment options that don't charge more than 1 percent annually, then consider signing up with the home team. If you decide later that it isn't the best plan for you, transfer to another 529 plan.

If you're leaning toward a Coverdell ESA but still have doubts, go ahead and open one. The funds can be transferred to a 529 plan without penalty. (However, the other way around—taking money from a 529 plan and putting it in a Coverdell ESA—will incur distribution penalties,

COLLEGE SAVINGS PLANS COMPARISON CHART

	Coverdell ESA	529: Prepaid Tuition	529: Savings Plan
Highlights	An investment account available to contributors who earn less than $110K (for single filers) and $220K (for joint filers)	Contributions today will cover tuition costs in the future	A state-sponsored investment account that benefits your child, your cousin, your neighbor, yourself
Offered by...	Brokerages, mutual fund companies, banks	States	States (with help from financial services companies)
Contribution limit	$2,000 per student per year	Depends on plan and age of student	Depends on plan—varies from $100,000 to $305,000
Tax treatment of withdrawals	Tax-free if used for qualified expenses	Tax-free if used for qualified expenses	Tax-free if used for qualified expenses until 2010 (distributions will count as income to the student in 2011 and beyond unless Congress extends the current law)
Qualified expenses	Tuition, room and board, fees, supplies, and special needs related to the attendance of a qualified elementary, secondary, or post-secondary institution	Tuition at a college within the plan (some plans will also cover room and board)	Tuition, fees, and room and board at qualified higher-education institutions
Tax-deductibility	None	Some states allow contributions to be partially or completely deductible	Some states allow contributions to be partially or completely deductible

continued...

COLLEGE SAVINGS PLANS COMPARISON CHART (continued)

	Coverdell ESA	529: Prepaid Tuition	529: Savings Plan
Investment flexibility	Assets can be invested in stocks, bonds, mutual funds, and cash equivalents. Investments can be bought and sold as often as desired.	Plan administrators invest all assets	Assets are professionally managed. Depending on the plan, participants can choose from up to almost 30 mutual fund-type investments. Investments may be changed once every 12 months.
Ability to transfer account	Account may be transferred to other brokerage or mutual fund, or to a 529 plan, subject to fees and penalties	Depends on plan	May transfer to another 529 plan once every 12 months
Effect on financial aid	Considered the student's asset (i.e., much of it will be considered in the financial aid calculation)	Considered the student's resource, thus reducing financial aid dollar for dollar	Assets are account owner's property. Unless the owner is also the beneficiary, only a small portion will be considered in the financial aid calculation.
Control of the account	In most states, control can remain with the "responsible individual" or be turned over to the student at the age of majority (18 to 21, depending on the state)	In most states, contributor retains control of account	In most states, contributor retains control of account
Must use funds by...	Age 30	Varies by plan	Varies by plan

continued...

COLLEGE SAVINGS PLANS COMPARISON CHART (continued)			
	Coverdell ESA	**529: Prepaid Tuition**	**529: Savings Plan**
Assignability to other relatives	Immediate family, including cousins, step-relatives, and in-laws	Immediate family, including cousins, step-relatives, and in-laws	Immediate family, including cousins, step-relatives, and in-laws
Penalty for non-qualified withdrawals	Earnings are taxed as ordinary income to contributor, plus a 10% penalty	Earnings are taxed as ordinary income to account owner, plus a 10% penalty	Earnings are taxed as ordinary income to account owner, plus a 10% penalty
Contribution deadline	Tax-filing deadline for the year of the contribution	Depends on plan	Depends on plan

and this won't get you around the $2,000 annual contribution limit.) You can switch later if additional research or financial aid considerations convince you that a 529 plan is better.

So don't dally—start saving *now*!

Five Fast Facts

1. There's a whole lotta aiding going on, roughly $90 billion of it annually.

2. Aid distribution is based primarily on the family's financial need, but also on the student's smarts, talent, and well-roundedness. Parents should position their finances so that they are eligible for more aid, and students should work hard at school, study for the standardized admissions tests, and get involved in several extracurricular activities (preferably ones that can be listed on a college application without breaking public-decency laws).

3. The vast majority of aid comes in the form of loans. While a college education is often worth the assumption of debt, factor the need for loans into your choice of schools.

4. The amount of aid you're offered is determined partially by set formulas, but a school's financial aid officers (especially those at private colleges) have a lot of latitude. If you think you deserve more, make your case personally.

5. You have to apply for financial aid for each year of attendance; this isn't a one-shot deal (unless you can figure out a way to earn a degree in 12 months). Find out how much of your aid you can expect to be renewed.

Financial Aid

With the price of education so high, surely schools don't expect you to pay that much without a little help...do they? Well, no, and yes.

Most financial aid is given as loans—not scholarships or grants—but don't let that deter you from trying to get a piece of the "free money" pie. To get a slice, you'll have to demonstrate need (show how your income and assets couldn't cover the cost of attendance without undue hardship) or exceptionality (prove how your intelligence, talents, ethnicity, gender, or background would make you an attractive addition to the student body), or both.

If you take just one lesson away from reading this book, let it be this: Don't smoke! It's harmful to your health and net worth, and it makes your breath stink.

And if you take away *two* lessons, here's the other: You don't have to be "needy" to get need-based aid. Many factors determine your eligibility for aid, such as the cost of attending a school, the number of family members in college, and how much the school wants you. So don't assume you won't be eligible for financial aid.

HOW NEED IS DETERMINED

Financial aid applicants must fill out several forms and reveal information about their family's income and assets. When this information is processed, out comes a magic number: the Expected Family Contribution (EFC). This is how much, according to formulas we'll soon discuss, your family should be able to contribute to a post-secondary education. Then, that amount is subtracted from the cost of attending a particular school, and— *voilà!*—the result is how much aid you'll need.

So, if it will cost $12,000 a year to attend a school, and your EFC is determined to be $7,000, you'll receive an aid package worth $5,000. If attendance will cost $30,000 annually, then your aid package will be worth $23,000. Simple as that...with these caveats:

- "Cost of attendance" includes tuition, room and board, textbooks, fees, and estimated living and travel expenses. How these costs are determined vary widely from school to school.

- Some schools practice "gapping," which means they won't offer an aid package that covers 100 percent of the difference between the cost of attendance and the EFC. So, you'll have to fill a "gap" between your EFC and their aid package.

Still, it's encouraging that, in most situations, a school will help you find a way to cover the costs.

HOW THE EFC IS CALCULATED
The process begins with the Free Application for Federal Student Aid (FAFSA), which comes to you courtesy of the Department of Education. How information on the FAFSA is turned into an EFC is a complicated process (known as the "federal methodology"), but we can reveal this much:

- The formula considers parental and student assets and income differently. Parents are expected to contribute up to 5.6 percent of their assets and up to 47 percent of their income toward their kid's education, whereas the student is expected to contribute 35 percent of assets and 50 percent of income. For this reason, it is almost always better to have college savings in the parents' name, not the student's.

- Generally, not all assets and income will be part of the equation. Income figures are reduced by the amount of taxes paid, and "protection allowances" shelter a portion of income and assets. (These protection allowances tend to be higher for parents—another reason to keep college savings in Mom and Dad's name.) Also, home equity and retirement assets are not counted.

- If more than one child will be getting an undergraduate education at the same time, the parents' portion of the EFC is split up among them. If the parents' expected contribution is $12,000 and they will have two kids in college, then the parents will be expected to pay $6,000 per child. This will qualify each student for more aid.

The majority of public institutions rely solely on the federal methodology, as do some private schools. And, all schools *must* use the federal methodology when distributing aid from Uncle Sam (which accounts for almost 70 percent of aid). But when it comes to handing out their own funds, many schools depend on information from the PROFILE form, which is administered by the College Board and required of applicants by many private institutions. (Some schools have their own forms.) Using this additional information, schools have their own way of calculating need, known as the "institutional methodology," and it differs from the federal methodology in several important respects:

- **Home equity:** The institutional methodology considers equity built up in your home. As some consolation, the mortgage on your primary residence is usually the only kind of debt some schools will take into account. (For this reason, some experts advise turning consumer debt, which isn't counted, into mortgage debt by paying off that credit card balance or car loan with a home equity loan.)

- **Student's income:** There is no "protection allowance" (i.e., income that's not part of the equation) for the student's income. A portion of every dollar he earns is expected to go toward the education bill.

- **Student's assets:** The institutional method factors in 25 percent of the student's assets, instead of the 35 percent considered under the federal method.

- **Parents' assets:** A smaller percentage of Mom and Dad's assets is considered fair game for the aid formula.

- **Retirement assets:** Some schools take into account money in the parents' tax-advantaged retirement accounts.

- **Siblings' assets:** A large amount of money owned by siblings can reduce aid eligibility.

- **Multiple kids in college:** Whereas the federal methodology divides the parents' EFC equally among their college-enrolled offspring, the institutional methodology figures parents will contribute 60 percent of their EFC for each student.

- **Coverdells, prepaid plans, and 529 savings plans:** Each of these accounts is treated differently in the federal methodology (see the "Financial aid factor" sections in the preceding chapters). However, the institutional method treats these accounts all the same, and all favorably. Assets in these accounts are considered as the parents', and will be assessed at a rate between 3 and 5 percent.

Remember that these are general practices. Each school has its own policies for distributing money, so get the skinny on the schools to which you're applying.

TYPES OF AID

As mentioned earlier, schools will try to pick up where your EFC leaves off. That's the good news. The not-as-good news is that, since most financial aid comes in the form of loans, most applicants can attend any school to which they're accepted, but they may graduate with thousands of dollars in debt. Is it worth it? That's a question we'll consider later, but let's first review what you might find when you open your bulging aid package.

Grants

The more grants make up your aid package, the more you should thank your lucky stars. This money is given and not expected to be returned. Free dough. It doesn't get any better than that.

Grants come in all shape and sizes, and from different sources. The most well-known federal version is the Pell grant, which is awarded to families that demonstrate exceptional financial need. Approximately 30 percent of undergraduate students receive a Pell grant. A similar grant is the Federal Supplemental Education Opportunity Grant (FSEOG), which also goes to lower-income families.

States also provide grants, often through an agency with the words "commission on higher education" in its name. These grants aren't just need-based. States will often award grants to residents who earned a respectable GPA in high school and attend in-state colleges (public or private). Some states determine who gets aid according to the FAFSA; others have their own forms. To find out what assistance is offered by your state—and what you need to do to get it—visit www.ed.gov/Programs/bastmp/SHEA.htm, ask your guidance counselor, or pay the governor's mansion a visit (bring cookies).

Schools also have their own resources from which to award grant money. But regardless of the source, the school decides who gets the grant money. Most federal grant money is sent to the school, which then distributes it until the well runs dry.

Work-study

With federal money, a school will pay a student to answer office phones, make copies for professors, or serve Sloppy Joes at the cafeteria. It's a job—and not a particularly well-paid one at that. The typical work-study award is between $1,000 and $1,500. While it is true that you can find better-paying jobs elsewhere, keep this in mind: Fifty percent of the income a student earns from a regular job (above the income-protection allowance of $2,200, as of 2002) goes toward the EFC for the following year, thus reducing aid eligibility. This is not true of a work-study job.

Loans

Who do you go to when you need money? Your rich uncle, of course—in this case, Uncle Sam. If you need to borrow money for school, you probably don't have to go to anyone else.

But regardless of where you got the money, there are several questions you should have answered before you sign the promissory note.

- **Is the loan subsidized?** If some other entity (usually the federal government) will pay the loan interest while the student is in school, then the loan is "subsidized." Otherwise, the interest is "capitalized" (i.e., added to the principal of the loan).

Capitalization significantly jacks up the cost of the loan because it increases its size, and the borrower essentially will be paying interest on the interest. So, if given the choice, always take the subsidized loan. Then, if possible, pay the interest while in school.

- **How often is the loan capitalized?** With unsubsidized loans, it's important to know how often unpaid interest will be added to the principal. Just once? Every year? The more times a loan is capitalized, the more money it will take the borrower to pay off the balance.

- **Will I get a break for paying on time?** If a loan is bought or issued by Sallie Mae (about a third of all school loans), the interest rate will be reduced by a quarter of a percentage point if the borrower authorizes the electronic debit of loan payments from a bank account. Those who pay on time for four years will see their interest rates reduced by a percentage point.

- **How much will it cost to originate the loan?** Most loans charge an origination fee (typically 3 percent), as well as a guarantor fee to insure against default (1 percent).

Here's the lowdown on loans typically available to students and their parents:

Perkins loans

Awarded to undergraduate and graduate students with exceptional need, this is the best school loan available. The interest rate is always 5 percent, and the government subsidizes the loan by paying the interest while the student is in school and nine months after graduation. There are no origination fees.

Additionally, Perkins loans can be canceled for graduates who choose certain jobs, such as a nurse, a law enforcement officer, an employee of a family-service agency, a Peace Corps volunteer, or a teacher. In some cases, the cancellation is available only if the borrower works in certain low-income communities, so check with the Department of Education for more information.

Stafford loans

These are government-subsidized loans to undergraduate and graduate students with financial need. Unsubsidized Stafford loans are available to all students, regardless of need. Stafford loans come in two flavors:

1. Federal Direct Student Loan Program (FDSLP): Provided by the U.S. government directly to borrowers, most commonly known as Direct loans.
2. Federal Family Education Loan Program (FFELP): Provided by private lenders but guaranteed by the federal government against default.

Which type of Stafford loan you're offered depends on the school. The terms of the Direct and FFELP loans are identical, so it doesn't matter which type your school offers.

PLUS loans

The Parent Loan for Undergraduate Students (PLUS) is available to parents of dependent students. Like Stafford loans, PLUS loans are either Direct or FFELP loans. The interest rates are higher than those on Perkins or Stafford loans, and repayment begins 60 days after the first tuition payment is made with loan funds.

Private loans

You should be able to borrow all you need from the federal student loan programs. The limits are often high enough to cover all your costs, and the terms are hard to beat. But there's nothing wrong with doing a little comparison-shopping. Start with Sallie Mae (www.salliemae.com), which—besides buying up loans from other lenders—offers its own loans. Other sources of private school loans are the Education Resources Institute (www.teri.org) and Nellie Mae (www.nelliemae.com). And there's always your local bank, credit union, or wealthy relative.

Private scholarships

There are entire books, and businesses, devoted to helping students get scholarships from sources outside the government and universities. Indeed, thousands of organizations—from service groups to multinational corporations—provide scholarship money. However, some

DON'T TAKE SCHOOL LOANS LIGHTLY

Most financial professionals say that taking on debt to earn a degree is a prudent move, and we generally agree. After all, college grads earn almost twice as much as their high-school grad counterparts. However, those loans could be a burden on your kid as she starts off her career. Here's an excerpt from an email we received:

> A friend of my wife's is a teacher and makes about $30,000 a year. She is a single mom with two kids, 6 and 2. Her youngest is profoundly deaf and will, of course, need extra financial support throughout his life. Her problem is that she has about $40,000 in college loans that are just beginning to come due. She is realizing that she will never be able to save anything and she will be burdened with these payments for a long time. Of course a house, decent car, etc., will also be out of her reach.

It's an extreme example, but it does demonstrate how burdensome school loans can be. According to a survey conducted by the Cambridge Consumer Credit Index, 67 percent of graduates with school loans say those loans prevent them from buying a car or a home. The State Public Interest Research Groups—an alliance of state-based public-interest advocates—says that 39 percent of borrowers graduate with debt that consumes 8 percent of their incomes. Also, students who don't graduate (the case with more than half of students who begin a degree program) still have to pay back the loans.

Should you eschew school loans? It depends. If it's the only way your child can go to college, the loans could be a great investment. But assuming any form of debt should never be taken lightly. If the difference between attending one school over another means taking on thousands of dollars' worth of loans, factor that prominently into your decision.

If money must be borrowed, the student should take out the loan, not the parents. Why? Because the loans offered to students (Stafford, Perkins) have lower interest rates and more deferment options than those available to parents. Also, it's possible the student will take a job with an employer who will pay off the loan. Finally, a student is more likely to be able to deduct the loan interest from his taxable income (see Appendix A: Education and Tax Breaks).

experts caution that students shouldn't spend too much time vying for scholarship money, because:

- Only 4 percent of financial aid comes from private scholarships, with the average award being approximately $1,600.

- Competition for some scholarships can be intense.

- Most schools will consider a scholarship as a student's resource—and thus reduce any need-based aid dollar for dollar. As a result, the scholarship may not save you any money because it ends up replacing a grant the school would have otherwise awarded you. Fortunately, this practice is changing at some schools, where scholarships will replace loans instead of grants. Before you spend time scouring for scholarships, know the policies of the schools to which you'll be applying.

Those are good points, but it still can be worthwhile to look for scholarships—especially if you don't expect to qualify for other forms of aid, or your package consists solely of loans. Just ask Ben Kaplan, who managed to amass almost $90,000 by winning more than two dozen scholarships. Granted, this guy got into Harvard, so he's no dummy. But the lessons he teaches in his book (*How to Go to College Almost for Free*) and on his website (www.scholarshipcoach.com) can be used by anyone.

To increase your chances of winning a scholarship, start local. You'll have a better chance of getting a scholarship for students in your city (which will have fewer applicants) than winning a nationwide competition. But don't ignore a national scholarship if you think you have a good chance. Also, start early—even before junior or senior years of high school. Many scholarships are open to students of all ages.

Where can you find scholarships? As with most of life's enduring mysteries, the best place to look for answers is the Internet. You can find free scholarship search services at CollegeBoard.com, FastWeb.com, WiredScholar.com, and FinAid.org. Also, check out books like *The Scholarship Book* by National Scholarship Research Service.

POSITION YOUR FINANCES FOR AID ELIGIBILITY

Looking to increase your chances for financial aid? There are many perfectly legal ways to put your finances in an uglier light—and the uglier your finances, the more need-based aid you might receive.

When it comes to rearranging your balance sheet, note this important principle: The income figures used in the various financial aid formulas are from the previous year, and the asset figure is as of the filing date.

For example, let's say your student will be a college freshman during the 2006-2007 academic year. As you complete the FAFSA (and other forms, if required), all questions about *income* will be about the previous year (2005). So, if you want to take steps to alter your income for optimal aid eligibility, you may have to do so before January of your student's junior year, before Father Time rings in 2005.

However, all answers to questions about *assets* will be based on your balance sheet as of the moment you sign the forms. So you have until you file your application to play with your assets.

Here are some possibly aid-enhancing strategies:

- **Don't sell any securities for a profit in the year before you apply for aid.** Any profits you see from sales of securities will be counted toward your income. Also, unless you've spent the proceeds of the sale, the profit will also show up among your assets, so they'll be counted twice.

- **Reduce income as much as possible.** If you have losses from lousy investments or a business venture gone wrong, the tax year before you apply for aid would be the time to take them.

- **If you anticipate making a big-ticket purchase, do it before applying for aid.** For example, if your car is on its last wheels, and you plan to buy a replacement soon, then do so before you sign the FAFSA in order to reduce your assets. If you're a renter and will be applying to schools that use only the federal methodology (i.e., don't factor in home equity), perhaps now is the time to become part of the landed gentry—and get thousands of dollars out of your bank or brokerage accounts. Note: You may not use this "make big-ticket purchases" strategy as an excuse to buy a recreational vehicle with a Jacuzzi.

- **Contribute to retirement accounts.** The federal methodology does not factor in retirement assets, so moving money from your bank account to an IRA will shelter some assets. And you should be saving for retirement anyhow. What, you think Social Security will take care of you? (Evil laughter fills the room.)

- **Use assets to pay off debt.** Not only is getting rid of consumer debt—such as credit card balances and car loans—good for your overall financial health, but doing so with extra cash lying around will reduce the assets used in financial aid formulas.

DON'T BE ORDINARY

As mentioned earlier, there are two ways to get financial aid: Show need and demonstrate exceptionality. We've already prattled on about the former, so let's discuss the latter.

Schools want a diverse, talented, and bright student body. This is not just out of principle; a school's reputation is largely formed by the quality of its students. Schools use attractive aid packages to increase the chances that ideal students will enroll, known as "preferential packaging." How can you make this work to your benefit? Do all you can to make yourself stand out. (Within reason, of course—keep your second navel and scratch-and-sniff tattoos under wraps.)

Here are some ways you can be extraordinary:

Your academics

This is the biggie. Schools covet smart kids. People who are accepted to the Harvards and Stanfords of the world are *all* smart, so you have to be super-duper smart to make your brains work to your advantage. Where academic success really pays off is at the so-called second- and third-tier schools—places that provide a very good education but don't quite have Yale's reputation. These schools will do a lot to entice brainy kids to enroll.

Your background

While most people think of affirmative action when they hear the word "diversity," the truth is that schools like a student body that hails from all kinds of places, races, and economic backgrounds.

Your talents and interests

Depending on the school, you may get some tuition relief from being a gifted artist or athlete. Leadership skills are also valued—some schools give scholarships to anyone who's been senior class president.

STRUTTING YOUR INTELLECTUAL STUFF

We can't overemphasize the importance of doing well in high school. An applicant's GPA, class rank, and standardized test scores will open many doors—both in terms of the quality of school that will accept him and the amount of aid offered. This is an area where a student can make a great contribution to lowering the cost of college.

It doesn't end once a student has been accepted to an undergraduate program. The GPA earned while obtaining a B.S. or B.A. will have an impact on the amount of aid offered if the student decides to pursue an M.A. or Ph.D.

But whether you are applying to an undergraduate or graduate program, the amount of merit-based aid you receive will depend on how much your record stands out among the rest of the applicant pool. You'll increase your chances by applying to schools where your academic record puts you in the top 25 percent of those vying for acceptance.

GET BUSY: APPLYING FOR, AND GETTING THE MOST, FINANCIAL AID

The following steps are based on a student entering an undergraduate institution straight from high school, but they also apply to students who take time off before going to college, as well as prospective graduate school students.

Step 1: From birth, make your kid smart

Start the brain-building process early. Play Mozart CDs, read great books aloud, and recite multiplication tables—and you should do even more once the baby exits the womb.

Step 2: Beginning in freshman year of high school, calculate your EFC regularly

You don't have to wait to receive your aid package to get an idea of what your EFC will be. There are several Web-based calculators that can give you an estimate. Give the tools at CollegeBoard.com, FinAid.com, or Kiplinger.com a whirl. With an estimate of how much you'll be expected to shell out, you can plan accordingly.

Step 3: Improve aid eligibility

Use the EFC calculators to see if employing a few eligibility-enhancing strategies might pay off. The income figures used are based on the tax year that begins January 1 of the junior year in high school, so you'll have to start making adjustments before then. However, you have until you sign your aid application forms to shift assets.

Step 4: Complete the FAFSA, PROFILE, and/or other forms as necessary

Ascertain the application deadlines from the schools to which you're applying, and—come Hel (the Norse queen of the underworld) or high water—do not miss them. The federal government will begin accepting FAFSAs on January 1 of the year a student expects to enter college. The FAFSA requires information from your tax return from the preceding year, so you'll have to complete your return beforehand. (You don't have to file your tax return then; you can just keep it until April 15 if you owe money.) If you have questions, call the Department of Education's Federal Student Aid Information Center at (800) 4-FED-AID.

Schools set their own application deadlines for the PRO-FILE and other forms. Some of these deadlines are before January 1, especially for students applying for early admission.

Financial aid forms—like Shakespearean insult generators, FindAGrave.com, and the Anagram Genius Server—can be found on the Internet. Visit www.fafsa.ed.gov to file your FAFSA online. Go to www.collegeboard.com to complete the PROFILE.

Step 5: Your EFC will be computed and sent to you and the schools you indicated

You will receive a Student Aid Report (SAR) within one to four weeks. The SAR will contain your EFC. Review the results for accuracy.

Step 6: Receive an aid package... then negotiate

Based on the information you provided and the policies they implemented, the schools to which your favorite applicant was accepted will send a fat envelope describing your aid package. You may not be stuck with the first aid package you're offered. It's not unreasonable to ask the financial aid office to take another look, but be very clear why you think they should reconsider. Here are some possible reasons:

- You want to make sure they are aware of extraordinary financial circumstances, such as outrageous medical bills, a recent loss of income, or having to care for elderly parents.

- You have received a much more generous offer from another school, and you'd like to give the school a chance to match it. Some financial aid officers are more receptive to this tactic than others.

- The forms you submitted weren't processed accurately, and you'd like to have your EFC recalculated. It's always possible that a FAFSA processor made a mistake, or your handwritten "$40,000" looks like "$90,000." Review all paperwork for accuracy and clarity.

- You received a one-time windfall (such as an inheritance) that skewed your results.

- You are paying for your other children to attend a private elementary or secondary school, or even grad school. Some schools (mostly private schools) will take into account other tuition bills.

- The student has been receiving Social Security benefits, which may have been included in the aid calculation. However, benefits end at age 18, so the student won't have that resource in college.

- You're just curious about how your EFC was calculated. Financial aid officers have a lot of leeway in how they distribute money. They often make judgments about an applicant's finances based on their experience and expertise. For example, there is more than one way to calculate a home's equity, and tax deductions might be added back to income. Ask for an explanation of how your aid was determined.

Step 7 : Accept the aid offer
You won't have forever to make up your mind. The school will give you a deadline by which you must accept the aid offered.

**ive
ast
acts**

1. The financial aid rigmarole for graduate school is very similar to what students must navigate to get aid for a bachelor's degree.

2. To save for graduate school, you can use a Coverdell ESA or a 529 savings plan or both.

3. The really plum aid for graduate school is used to attract outstanding students, so an admirable academic record will increase your chances for free money.

4. If you play your cards right, you may get not just a break on tuition, but also a stipend or a part-time job with the university.

5. Many government agencies and private groups are willing to help graduate students. Search for aid from organizations related to your field of study.

Chapter 8

Paying for Graduate School

In this chapter...
- Make them want you
- Where to find fellowships and assistantships
- Master's degree or doctorate?
- Find the funds

Did you earn your undergraduate degree years ago, but you're tired of working for a living? Or maybe you're about to complete your bachelor's degree, and you want to delay your entry into the 9-to-5 world as long as possible? Then graduate school might be for you!

But seriously, folks... Graduate school could be your ticket to broadened skills, expanded opportunities, and a higher income.

Paying for a graduate education has a lot in common with financing a bachelor's degree. To wit:

- Savings in a Coverdell ESA or a 529 plan can be used for qualified graduate school costs. (However, contributions can't be made to a Coverdell after the beneficiary turns 18, and the money in the account must be used by the time the beneficiary reaches 30.)

- Billions of dollars await to make a degree more affordable.

- Financial aid is awarded based on need and talent. The less money and more brains you have, the more aid you'll receive.

- The financial aid application processes for undergraduate and graduate students share many similarities, so if you skipped the riveting discussion of the ins and outs of the financial aid world, go back to the previous chapter and take copious notes.

Yet, as you might suspect, there are important differences. The biggest are:

- Grad students can be awarded a special kind of scholarship, called a "fellowship"—the Holy Grail of post-graduate financial aid.

- Grad schools offer a different kind of work-study: assistantships. In exchange for a tuition waiver and a stipend, you'll lend a helping hand (and brain) to the school.

- Pell grants and PLUS loans are not available to grad students.

- Academic achievement, standardized test scores, and recommendations from teachers are even more important to getting aid as a grad student.

- The department to which you are accepted has a lot of control over the aid that is disbursed.

- When it comes to applying for financial aid, most undergrads are considered their parents' dependents, so Mom and Dad's assets and income become a factor. However, grad students, who are considered independent, are judged based on their own assets and income.

- Grad schools usually charge higher tuition rates.

- There's no need for a fake I.D.

Let's take a more detailed look at how paying for graduate school is a unique adventure.

MAKE THEM WANT YOU

The department in which you'll study has a lot of control over who gets aid. Because professors work more closely with grad students than they do with undergrads, they have a greater interest in who enrolls in their graduate programs. Accordingly, the department will use aid packages to attract the better students.

Therefore, it's important to make yourself as attractive as possible—and we're not talking about a tummy tuck or nose job. We're talking about a good GPA, an outstanding score on standardized tests such as the Graduate Record Exam (GRE) or the Graduate Management Admission Test (GMAT), and recommendations from wildly impressed professors.

FELLOWSHIPS

Fellowships, like scholarships, are awards of free money given to students who demonstrate exceptional academic ability or, in some cases, financial need. They can come in the form of a tuition waiver, a stipend, or both.

Some fellowships are for first-year students only. Others are renewable. Some are guaranteed for a number of years. Make sure you know the details about any fellowships you're awarded.

ASSISTANTSHIPS

Want a job? Then an assistantship is for you! In exchange for a stipend, reduced tuition, or both, you'll spend approximately 20 hours a week grading exams, conducting research, or even teaching undergraduate courses. About 60 percent of graduate students at large public schools get some aid through assistantships.

Because an assistantship is a job, some students take on a lighter course load. But the opportunity to get experience in your field and hobnob with faculty members is often well worth taking longer to get a degree.

As with fellowships (and all aid, really), verify how long it will last. Also, find out if you will be considered an employee of the university and whether you'll be eligible for benefits.

WHERE TO FIND FELLOWSHIPS AND ASSISTANTSHIPS

Begin your quest for graduate goodies at these sources:

- The department to which you're applying

- The school's financial aid office (if you have the right experience, you might be able to secure an assistantship in another department)

- Any of the numerous books that list fellowships and scholarships

- If you'll be attending a school in your home state, check with your state's commission on higher education

A MASTER'S DEGREE OR A DOCTORATE?

When it comes to doling out funds, schools tend to give more aid to doctoral students. After all, it usually takes just two or three years to earn a master's degree, whereas a doctorate can take almost a decade. Therefore, Ph.D. candidates need more aid.

If you are undecided as to whether to go for a master's or doctorate, apply for the latter. You will likely get more aid. If you decide not to pursue it, you won't be required to return any of the aid you received. It goes without saying that you should only apply to a doctoral program if you are sincerely interested—but we felt the need to say it, anyway.

- Government agencies, research organizations, and private associations related to your field of study (www.students.gov is a good place to begin your search)

ODDS AND ENDS

- To save on room and board (and perhaps on tuition), see if the school employs grad students as residence hall administrators. You'd probably have to live in a dorm and manage undergraduate resident assistants, but you'd be close to campus and rediscover the delicacies of cafeteria food.

- If you attend a public university but you're not a resident, find out what it takes to become one (and pay the in-state tuition).

- Sometimes your employer will help with financial aid. In this case, you will often have to continue working at your job.

- There's always the classic fallback: debt. Stafford loans are available to grad students, complete with higher borrowing limits than those available to undergrads. Before taking out loans worth thousands (and perhaps tens of thousands) of dollars, factor in the amount of debt into your choice of school—and whether getting the degree is worth owing so much money.

GET BUSY: FIND THE FUNDS FOR GRADUATE SCHOOL

The pursuit of post-undergrad funding is dictated largely by your area of study. Students attending medical school will face a completely different scenario than those getting their Ph.D. in English Literature. So, more field-specific research will pay off. However, these steps apply to most aspiring graduate students:

Step 1: Kick academic arse as an undergrad

The higher your GPA and the more effusive the recommendations from your professors, the more your chances of being awarded a fellowship, assistantship, or scholarship. Doing well on the requisite standardized tests will also boost your stock.

Step 2: Understand the financial aid process

Undergraduate and graduate students have a lot in common, at least when it comes to financing an education.

Many of the tips contained in the previous chapter—how to increase eligibility for need-based aid, how to find private scholarships—also apply to paying for graduate school.

Step 3: Search high and low for people who want to give you money

Talk to the people in your department and in the financial aid office at your school. Search the Internet. Peruse books that list fellowships and scholarships. But whatever you do, be mindful of deadlines. Every distributor of aid abides by its own calendar.

Five Fast Facts

1. If you haven't saved enough to cover the costs of college, don't despair. There are ways to lower the price tag.

2. Though your degree will come from just one school, you don't have to take all your classes there. Find cheaper ways to take the general requirements or elective classes, then transfer those credits to the school that will confer the degree.

3. Use the Internet to cut costs, by buying used textbooks or taking classes online.

4. Coverdell ESAs and 529s are relatively recent creations. For years, parents relied on other strategies to pay for school, such as investing in custodial accounts and taking out home equity loans. Some of these old methods still have merit, whereas others are past their prime.

5. Uncle Sam doesn't just give out money for school. He also provides career opportunities that offer enticing educational benefits.

Chapter 9

Money-Saving Tips and Alternative Strategies

In this chapter...
- Lower the price tag
- Help from Uncle Sam
- Alternative strategies
- Borrowing against your home or life insurance

So you haven't saved enough to pay for your kid's college? Well, if it's any consolation, you're not alone. A study by Sallie Mae found that parents of high schoolers applying for college had saved less than half of what they needed to cover their expected expenses. What's more, one in five hadn't saved anything at all.

Of course, you may have been saving for years, but you're still looking for ways to cut college costs. Consider these money-saving tips:

Make sure your little Socrates is *really* ready to go to college
Less than half of students at four-year colleges actually graduate. Before plunking down (or borrowing) thousands of dollars, make sure that this is something your child wants to do.

Choose a cheaper school
Weigh carefully the benefits of a private school against the cost savings offered by a larger state school. Would a psychology degree from Snooty U. really be more valuable than one from State U.? Is the honor worth 10 years of debt?

Attend a school close to home
As an in-state student at a public institution, your student will pay a reduced tuition and be eligible for financial aid earmarked for townies. Travel expenses and long-distance phone bills add up, especially during the first year when homesickness may be more pronounced than later (when your kid realizes that he doesn't really miss you that much after all). And do we dare suggest the student live at home?

Consider a community college for general requirements
Taking general courses and electives at a community college for the first year or two can save you 50 to 90 percent. Before doing so, however, find out if those courses will be accepted by the four-year schools to which you'd like them to transfer.

Look for co-op/intern programs

Many schools offer programs that allow students to go to school for one semester and then work in his field for a semester. It may take him a little longer to finish his degree, but when he gets out he'll have gained experience in his area of study. He'll also have some money in his pocket, and possibly a job offer from the company where he interned (assuming he didn't get caught putting itching powder on the toilet seats).

Cut housing costs

When you live on campus and eat at the school cafeteria, you pay for the convenience. It might be cheaper to live in someone's basement apartment and cook your own food. Or look for ways for the school to cover part or all of your room and board. The most common way to do this is to become a resident assistant.

Use the Internet to get cheaper textbooks

You don't have to pay $100 for that economics textbook. There are many used-book marketplaces on the Internet—such as Half.com, Amazon.com, and eCampus.com. The sooner you act, the greater your chances of getting a good deal. If you know in June which classes you'll take in September, start looking immediately—when the selection is bigger and the prices better.

Take classes online

Hundreds of colleges and universities now offer classes over the Internet. These programs are often called "distance learning" or "independent study." Most charge

EVEN MORE HELP FROM UNCLE SAM

Besides all the grants and loans provided by the federal government, there are other ways to get Uncle Sam to foot the bill. Some examples:

- **ROTC:** The United States Army, Navy, and Air Force operate Reserve Officers' Training Corps (ROTC) programs. ROTC scholarships, which are awarded based on academic and leadership ability, can cover two or four years' worth of college costs, plus a monthly stipend. Upon graduation, awardees must serve in the military for a certain number of years, which—depending on the program—can be a combination of serving active and reserve duty.

- **United States service academies:** You've heard of these places—West Point, Annapolis, the Air Force Academy. They are some of the most prestigious institutions in the country, and only the cream of the crop get accepted. The government bears all costs, and graduates must serve active duty for several years. Attending a service academy is more than a way to get a free education; it's a way of life. The programs are academically and physically rigorous, requiring a high level of dedication and determination. But who else would you want defending the country?

- **Montgomery GI Bill, Army College Fund, and College Loan Repayment:** These programs offer ways to defray future education expenses, or pay off federally insured school loans in exchange for enlistment.

- **AmeriCorps:** If you have a yen to work in disadvantaged communities, AmeriCorps may be for you. Members tutor and mentor young folks, clean up the environment, build affordable housing, and perform a host of other worthy jobs. In return, they receive (as of 2002) $4,725 to pay for school or pay off loans.

- **The Peace Corps:** If you're interested in joining the Peace Corps and pursuing a graduate degree, you can do both at the same time, while also reducing your education expenses. The Peace Corps offers programs that help cover the costs of graduate school or allow work experience to count as classroom credit.

- **Loan forgiveness:** Many programs will find a way to get your federal loans forgiven in exchange for working for non-profits or disadvantaged populations for a few years. The National Association for Public Interest Law and the National Health Service Corps, for example, sponsor such programs.

- **Scholarship, loans, and internships through individual agencies:** Many government bodies have devised ways to help former or future students cover the costs of education in exchange for service. To explore the possibilities, contact the agency that operates in a field that interests you.

Some of these programs can significantly reduce the cost of college. Others are a way to combine a desire to make a meaningful contribution with modest education benefits. Regardless of the economic rewards, you'll learn more about such programs at www.students.gov.

in-state tuition whether you're a resident of that state or not, and some charge even less than regular tuition. Even if you're enrolled in School A, you can take a few online classes from School B that will count toward your degree. However, make sure this is acceptable to School A beforehand.

Take advantage of AP and CLEP

Doing well on high school Advanced Placement (AP) exams can provide college credit before you even set foot on campus. And the College Board's College-Level Examination Program (CLEP) allows students of all ages (not just adults) to earn college credit by demonstrating proficiency in any of more than 30 subjects. But before you put your knowledge of French, Calculus, or Accounting to the test, make sure your college accepts CLEP credit.

ALTERNATIVE STRATEGIES

Putting money in a 529 plan or borrowing lots of money aren't the only ways to pay for school. There are other places to put those dollars, and other sources of loans. Many of the options we'll discuss here aren't the best ways to pay for school, but they've been around for a long time, and—before the relatively recent advent of Coverdell ESAs and 529 plans—were the only options available. Keep in mind that we're providing just the basics. If any of these ideas tickle your fancy, then make sure to do much more research.

Custodial accounts (UGMA and UTMA)

The UGMA and UTMA (not to be confused with the classic cheer "U-G-L-Y, you ain't got no alibi, you ugly, you ugly") stand for Uniform Gifts to Minors Act and Uniform Transfer to Minors Act, which govern these accounts. Using one of these accounts, money can be put in a minor's name, usually to gain some tax benefits. Despite the use of the term "uniform," the rules for these accounts vary from state to state (including whether the custodial account available to you is an UGMA or an UTMA). So, before you run off to grunt "UGMA" or "UTMA" at your broker, check your state laws. The accounts are very similar, except that UTMA accounts let the custodian maintain control over the money for a longer period of time—for example, until the child finishes college. Also, unlike the UGMA, the UTMA account can be invested in real estate, royalties, patents, and paintings.

Pros

- Until the child reaches 14, the first $750 in earnings are tax-free, and the next $750 in earnings are taxed at 10 percent (a rate lower than most parents' tax rate). All earnings beyond the first $1,500 are taxed at the parents' tax rate.

- At age 14, the child begins filing his own tax return. Unless the kid makes a killing in his lawn-mowing enterprise, the money will be taxed at the lowest tax bracket.

Cons

- As discussed in Chapter 7, assets owned by the student have a greater negative effect on financial aid eligibility than those owned by the parents.

- Once the child reaches the age of majority, she can do whatever she wants with the money.

- The funds must be used for the minor's benefit. Education expenses are proper uses of these assets; a big-screen TV for the family is not. (To keep out of trouble, keep records and receipts documenting the use of custodial assets.)

- Money deposited in an UGMA or UTMA is an irrevocable gift. Once it's there, you can't take it back.

If a student has money in an UGMA or UTMA, most states will allow that money to be transferred to a 529 plan, possibly reaping tax benefits and enhancing financial aid eligibility. However, a 529 account with money from a custodial account becomes the student's property at the age of majority, and she can do whatever she wishes with it. Plus, it can't be transferred to someone else's 529 plan. For this reason, you should open two 529 accounts, one funded by the UGMA/UTMA money and the other by contributions from other sources. Also, keep in mind that only cash can be contributed to a 529 plan, so any investments in the UGMA/UTMA will have to be sold, which may bring tax consequences.

Borrowing against your home

Using your home as collateral is a tried-and-true way to borrow money. There are two variations on this theme: lines of credit and loans (also known as second mortgages). With a home equity credit line, you are approved for a certain amount, and you borrow from it whenever necessary. A home equity loan, on the other hand, provides a lump sum of money that is repayable over a fixed period.

Pros

- As with the interest on your primary mortgage, the interest on a home equity loan or line of credit is tax-deductible in most cases (but make sure this applies to you beforehand).

- Since this loan is secured (i.e., backed by a tangible asset), the rates on home equity-based loans are better than those on many other loans.

- If your school includes home equity as an asset in financial aid calculations, the equity will probably be offset by mortgage debt. Therefore, borrowing against your home will reduce the amount of equity used to determine your financial aid.

Cons

- You are putting up your house as collateral for the loan. If for some reason you can't pay back the money, the bank can take your house.

- With a second mortgage, the bank gives you one lump sum, and you must begin paying it back immediately. If you don't use the entire sum, you'll be paying interest on money sitting in your bank account.

- Like any debt, borrowing against your home will leave less money for other purposes. This may compromise your other goals, especially retirement.

Borrowing from your life insurance policy

If you have a cash-value life insurance policy—or any of its variants, such as whole life, universal life, or variable life—you can borrow against any cash value built up in the policy.

Pros

- The "investment" portion of the policy grows tax-deferred.

- You can withdraw the amount you paid as premiums.

- The value of life insurance policies is sheltered from most financial aid calculations.

Cons

- Cash value life insurance policies usually suffer from very high expenses and commissions.

- When you "graduate" from this life, the policy's death benefit will be reduced by the value of any outstanding loans.

- The interest rates on insurance policy loans are not as attractive as those on most government-provided school loans or home equity loans.

- The "investment" portion of cash-value policies often offers horrendous returns.

- If you bail out within a few years of beginning the policy, surrender charges will be deducted from any cash value.

Tapping retirement funds

Money can be withdrawn from an IRA (individual retirement account) for higher-education expenses (tuition, room and board, books). Should you take advantage of these options? Not if you want to have money in retirement (and we think you do).

Pros

- Withdrawals are exempt from the 10 percent penalty for taking money out before the account owner is age 59½. Withdrawals from a traditional IRA, and the withdrawal of earnings from a Roth IRA that's been open less than five years, will be subject to income tax. (Contributions to a Roth IRA, as opposed to earnings, can be withdrawn tax- and penalty-free at any time, for any reason.)

Cons

- That money was intended to fund your golden years, not your children's education. If you use it to pay the tuition bill, you won't have that money when you retire, and you'll have missed out on the earnings that money could have generated over the years.

- If you don't have enough money to retire, you can't apply for financial aid. There's no such thing as a geezer scholarship. However, if your student doesn't have enough money to pay for school, he can apply for aid and take out a loan.

- The withdrawal will increase your income, which will increase your tax bill and reduce aid eligibility for the following year. Some experts suggest borrowing from a 401(k) as an alternative, since the loan won't affect your income. However, you're still compromising your retirement, and if you don't repay the loan (usually within five years), it's considered a distribution, subject to taxes and penalties.

Government savings bonds

Two types of government savings bonds offer some tax advantages when they're used to pay for qualified higher-education expenses: I Bonds and Series EE Bonds.

The I Bond's return is a combination of a fixed rate (established at the time of purchase) and a floating rate that is adjusted every six months based on the Consumer Price Index for all Urban users (CPI-U). Therefore, the return will keep up with inflation—which is what the "I" in I Bond stands for.

Series EE Bonds issued in January 1990 or later pay an interest rate based on the average yields for the preceding six months on five-year Treasury securities. The

rate is adjusted every six months. EE Bonds are purchased at half their face value (e.g., you pay $50 for a
$100 bond) but are guaranteed to reach face value in 17
years—a 4.24 percent annual return. You must be at least
24 years old to purchase bonds. If the future student is
younger than 24, then the bonds must be registered in
the parents' name.

Pros

- Because these securities are issued by the U.S. government, they are not taxable at the state level.

- Securities backed by Uncle Sam are the safest investments in the world.

- Taxes on Series EE Bonds and I Bonds can be de-
  ferred, and can be tax-free if used for qualified
  higher-education expenses.

- They can be purchased commission-free at
  www.treasurydirect.gov.

Cons

- The rate of return on government securities is not
  impressive. If you won't need the money for several years, you can probably do better with other
  investments.

- The tax-free status of interest on bonds used for
  education expenses is available only to those
  under certain income limits. For 2002, the portion

of interest that will be tax-free begins to decrease for single taxpayers with a modified adjusted gross income of $57,600, and is eliminated at a modified gross income of $72,600 and higher. Those numbers are $86,400 and $116,400, respectively, for married persons who file a joint return. The income limits will be adjusted every year for inflation.

- The expenses must be incurred in the same year that the bond is redeemed, so you'll have to co-ordinate your redemptions and tuition payments.

- The tax-free status on interest applies only if the bonds are used to pay for tuition and fees. Books and room and board are not eligible.

- A penalty equivalent to three months' worth of interest will be assessed if bonds are held for less than five years.

THE LOTTERY

Winning the super-duper-grande jackpot sure would go a long way to paying for college—you may even be able to buy your own college. But first, let's test your skills. Pick a number between 1 and 14 million.

Did you pick 9,747,384? You didn't? Well, perhaps you just don't have what it takes to win the lottery. Don't feel bad, though. Very few people do. You have just a one-in-14-million chance of winning. You have a greater chance of getting struck by lightning, though that won't help you pay for school (unless you can find a way to sue Mother Nature).

Five Fast Facts

1. If school is more than 10 years away, there's enough time to ride out the volatility of the stock market, and potentially earn a better return. As the student nears college enrollment, the money should be moved to safer investments (bonds and cash) so that by the college years, all money earmarked for education should be in cash equivalents (money market accounts, Treasury notes, certificates of deposit).

2. Start saving as soon as possible. Time is one of the greatest allies of the successful investor.

3. Administrative fees, management fees, commissions, and taxes are the bane of investors. Keep them to an absolute minimum.

4. One of the best ways to keep costs down—and achieve a respectable return—is to invest in index funds.

5. Though it's important to consider where to invest your money, the amount you can regularly put away in tax-advantaged college savings accounts will have a far greater impact on the ultimate value of your education nest egg. So, instead of spending lots of time looking for the best investments, find ways to live below your means and increase your savings rate.

Investing for School

Imagine a boy (let's call him Bam-Bam) who is born in 1980 and will go to college in 1998. During the intervening 18 years, Bam-Bam's parents save for college. Not trusting the fickle stock market, they put all their money in certificates of deposit. The result: Their money earned a return that was just a few percentage points above inflation, while they missed out on the greatest bull market in history.

Now imagine a girl (we'll call her Pebbles) born a few years later who, by the year 2000, is a high school sophomore. Her parents weren't particularly big believers in the stock market—until the mid-'90s. They rode the market up, and the size of Pebbles' college savings reflected it. In fact, they were so pleased with the results of their stock investments that they didn't diversify, even when Pebbles was just a couple of years from college. The result: Sixty percent of their college savings was wiped out by the vicious bear market that began in 2000 and continued for years.

While the biggest determinant of the size of your college savings is how much you regularly set aside, where you put your money will also have a say in the matter. When it comes to college savings, there's a time to go for growth, and a time to seek safety. This chapter will discuss fundamental and Foolish principles of investing, starting with the basic types of investments—what the highfalutin' folks call "asset classes."

CASH EQUIVALENTS

These types of investments offer secure ways to protect your money and earn a tiny bit of interest. You won't make much, but you probably won't lose anything, either. The most popular types of cash equivalents are money market investments, certificates of deposit, and Treasury bills. From 1926 to 2001, U.S. Treasury bills have averaged an annual return of 3.9 percent.

BONDS

Bonds are IOUs from governments and corporations. When a company issues a bond and an investor buys it, that investor is lending the company money. In return, the company will pay the investor a certain amount of money, known as interest. After a specified period, the company will return the investor's money.

A bond issued by the U.S. government is considered the safest investment in the world. There is very little chance that Uncle Sam won't be able to pay his bills. Corporate bonds are a little riskier—but they also pay more than a Treasury bond. Overall, bonds are considered pretty safe investments. Since 1926, long-term government bonds have averaged a return of 5.2 percent per year.

STOCKS

When you own a share of a company's stock, you own a piece of that company. There are two ways shareholders are rewarded for their ownership:

1. The company might pay a dividend. Shareholders receive a share of the company's profits. Some companies pay significant dividends; others don't, preferring instead to invest that money in new equipment, more research, or acquisitions.
2. The price of the stock might go up. Just like baseball cards and beaver pelts, stocks are traded in a marketplace, subject to the laws of supply and demand. As a company's earnings rise, more people want a piece of the action, spurring an increase in demand and in the price of the stock.

Stocks have been the best-performing long-term investment out there. But in the short term, the price of a stock can go down quickly—and stay down for years. Therefore, the only money that should be in the stock market is money you won't need for five years or more. From 1926 to 2001, large-company stocks have averaged a return of 10.2 percent per year, with years as bad as -43.59 percent and as good as +52.83 percent.

WHERE YOU SHOULD PUT YOUR MONEY

When it comes to college savings, your choice of investments—and how you purchase those investments—depends on the type of account you choose. So let's start with what's available in each college savings vehicle:

- **Prepaid tuition plans.** There is just one choice when it comes to prepaid tuition plans: Are you gonna sign up, or not? That's it. Once you send in the money, all the investment decisions are up to the managers of the plan.

- **529 savings plans.** Similar to prepaid plans, the money in a 529 savings plan is "professionally managed," i.e., a financial services firm employs managers to choose individual stocks and bonds. Within the plan, you are offered a choice of several funds. You decide what percentage of your contributions should go into the plan's stock fund, bond fund, and/or money market fund. (These categories are often broken into more specialized categories, such as international stocks or long-term bonds. If you're new to investing, stick to large American stock funds and short- to inter-

HOW TO EVALUATE A MUTUAL FUND

- Check the 5- and 10-year (if possible) history of the fund. What happened in the past will not necessarily happen in the future, but a fund's track record gives some hint of what a fund's manager can do. Avoid looking at the one- or three-year performance of a fund. Last year's winner is often this year's loser.

- Compare the fund's performance to other funds with the same objective. For example, if you're evaluating a corporate bond fund, compare it to other corporate bond funds. Do not compare it to government bond funds or stock funds.

- Look at the expenses charged by the fund. The average fund has an "expense ratio" (how much the fund charges each year) of 1.5 percent. If you can find a good fund that charges just 0.5 percent a year, you have added one percentage point to the return on your investments.

- Consult a source that evaluates funds. Morningstar, the best-known source of information about mutual funds, provides analysis, ratings, and performance history. Check it out at your library, or visit Morningstar.com.

If you decide to invest in stocks, then your choice of which stock fund is very easy. Look for the total market index fund.

An index is a set of stocks that a group of smarty-pants experts thinks represents a specific market, economy, or industry. Perhaps the most famous is the Dow Jones Industrial Average, which is a group of 30 stocks that the editors of *The Wall Street Journal* think represents the overall U.S. economy.

continued...

...continued

Another well-known index is the Standard & Poor's 500 Index, which most folks consider a good indicator of how the overall U.S. stock market is doing. Most index funds attempt to match it by buying each stock in the S&P 500, rather than hiring a manager to pick the stocks.

Why? Because most mutual funds can't beat the overall stock market, which also means that most mutual funds can't beat a total market index fund. In fact, if you invest in an index fund, you will likely outperform 70 to 80 percent of all other stock mutual funds over the long run.

This occurs for many reasons, but possibly the biggest reason is lower costs: An index fund doesn't pay a team of managers and analysts to pick the investments, which significantly lowers the costs of operating the fund. This means more of the money goes to the fund's shareholders—that's you!

mediate-term bond funds.) Many 529 plans also offer an "age-based portfolio." Contributions are automatically spread among the stock, bond, and money market funds, according to the student's age. As the student grows up, money is automatically transferred to safer investments. By the time the student graduates from high school, the age-based portfolio would have moved most of the money into bond and money market funds.

- **Coverdells, UGMAs, UTMAs, and other accounts.** These offer the most investment flexibility. You can buy whatever you want: a stock in

AGE-BASED PORTFOLIOS

Plan	Allocation for infants and toddlers ("The drooling years")	By the time high school rolls around ("The hormone hysteria years")	Allocation by freshman year of college ("The euphoric empty nest years")
West Virginia's SMART 529 Plan	100% stocks	50% stocks, 50% bonds	20% stocks, 80% bonds
Texas' Tomorrow's College Investment Plan	90% stocks, 10% bonds	50% stocks, 30% bonds, 20% money markets	15% stocks, 40% bonds, 45% money markets
Education Plan of New Mexico	85% stocks, 15% bonds	55% stocks, 40% bonds, 5% money markets	20% stocks, 40% bonds, 40% money markets
California's Golden State ScholarShare College Savings Trust	80% stocks, 20% bonds	30% stocks, 60% bonds, 10% money markets	20% stocks, 30% bonds, 50% money markets

General Electric, a bond offered by Ford, a real estate mutual fund, or a certificate of deposit, just to name a few of the thousands of possibilities.

Knowing what choices are available to you, the next question is, "What portion of my money should be in stocks, bonds, and cash?" This is known as "asset allocation"—how many eggs should go in which baskets.

To answer that question, let's return to the topic of age-based portfolios, which are offered by many 529 savings plans. Above are some examples.

As you can see, there is some slight variance, but the plans are generally in agreement: Stick with stocks in the early years, but be mostly in bonds and money markets by midway through high school. We could quibble with some of the numbers. Our biggest point of contention would be whether *any* money should be in stocks by the time the student goes to college; that's money needed in less than five years, so it fails the "Don't put short-term money into stocks" test. And some equity fans might argue that it's too conservative to put any money in bonds when little Galileo is still in diapers.

On the whole, though, we concur with the portfolio principles practiced by most age-based portfolios:

- Invest mostly in stocks when the kid is young.

- By the student's freshman year in high school, the portfolio should be divided equally (give or take) between stocks and bonds.

- Each year thereafter, move a third of the stock portfolio into bonds and cash equivalents. Depending on your investing savvy and risk tolerance, you should have little to no money in equities by the time you send in that first tuition payment.

GET BUSY: HOW TO INVEST FOR SCHOOL

If you're not comfortable with your knowledge of investing, then go conservative. The return on your

THE SECRETS TO INVESTING SUCCESS

- **Start early.** A parent who has 10 years to come up with $20,000 can do so by investing $109 a month (assuming an 8 percent annual return). Someone who has just five years to scrounge up 20 grand must sock away $271 a month—well more than twice as much.

- **Keep costs low.** Every dollar you pay to a broker or manager is a dollar less you have to grow through the years.

- **Find tax-friendly places for your money.** The less that goes to Uncle Sam, the more you can spend on tuition (and the less you may have to borrow).

- **Do it yourself...if you can.** If you need financial advice, you can get it, but it is rarely cheap. There's a reason why the median income for financial planners was $110,025 in 2001, according to the Financial Planning Association.

investments usually won't determine the size of your college savings account as much as the amount you manage to put away each month (except for investments solely in notorious bankruptcies such as WorldCom or Enron). So, don't fret inordinately much about investment returns; expend that energy on finding ways to save more money.

Step 1: Choose your college savings account(s) now!

Time is an investor's greatest ally. Don't spend a lot of time debating which broker's Coverdell, or which state's 529 plan, or which asset allocation is absolutely, positively the best. Do a reasonable amount of research, but then start saving immediately.

Step 2 : Learn more about investing

If you're a novice investor, start by putting money in something you're comfortable with, then expand your horizons. We've heard of this place called The Motley Fool (www.Fool.com) that offers user-friendly investment education, not to mention employees who can set a dance floor aflame.

Step 3 : Determine an asset allocation

Many studies have shown that how an investor divvies up his portfolio among the asset classes affects performance more than the choice of individual securities within each class. Make sure your asset allocation is appropriate for your time horizon.

Education and Tax Breaks

Besides the tax advantages of Coverdell ESAs and 529 plans, Uncle Sam offers a few other ways to take the sting out of paying for school. More specifically, there are ways to offset college costs with tax deductions and credits. The information provided here is meant merely to alert you to these opportunities. You should do *much* more research before including any of these breaks on your tax return. You can start by visiting www.Fool.com/taxes.

STUDENT-LOAN INTEREST DEDUCTION

If your income is below a certain limit ($65,000 for single taxpayers and $130,000 for married folks in 2002, though they are subject to change), you can deduct from your federal income tax the interest you pay on your school loan, up to $2,500 annually. This is an "above the line" deduction, i.e., you don't have to itemize your deductions to reap the benefit. So, if you otherwise qualify, you can claim the student-loan interest deduction even if you use the standard deduction.

HIGHER-EDUCATION EXPENSE DEDUCTION

Up to $3,000 can be deducted for qualified higher-education expenses that you pay for yourself, your spouse, or your family members. This $3,000 deduction comes into play in 2002 and 2003. In 2004 and 2005, the deduction is increased to $4,000. But, as with virtually all other education provisions, there are income limitations. You can kiss this deduction goodbye if your income exceeds $65,000 ($130,000 for married filers) in 2002 and 2003. Those income limitations increase to $80,000 ($160,000 for married filers) in 2004 and 2005. What happens in 2006? Unless legislation is passed that would make this provision permanent, it will be automatically repealed at the end of the 2005 tax year.

Be careful if you plan to use this deduction, since there are restrictive provisions that will not allow for the deduction if you also claim HOPE or Lifetime Learning credits in the same year for the same student. Restrictions also apply if you take distributions from a 529 plan.

EMPLOYER-PROVIDED EDUCATION ASSISTANCE

Your employer can pay for up to $5,250 of your qualified education expenses (undergraduate or post-graduate education) and you don't have to treat any of those payments as compensation or taxable income.

THE HOPE SCHOLARSHIP CREDIT

The HOPE Scholarship Credit allows taxpayers below certain income limits ($51,000 for single filers, $82,000 for joint filers in 2002) to convert part of the higher-education expenses you pay for yourself, your spouse, or your dependents into tax savings. The maximum HOPE credit a taxpayer may claim is $1,500 per year per student for the first two years of undergraduate education at an eligible educational institution. The credit equals the sum of:

- 100 percent of the first $1,000 of qualified tuition and related expenses paid, plus

- 50 percent of the next $1,000 of qualified tuition and related expenses paid.

The maximum HOPE credit amount will be adjusted for inflation beginning in 2002.

THE LIFETIME LEARNING CREDIT

The Lifetime Learning Credit has many similarities with the HOPE credit, but a few major differences. Here are the similarities:

- The school or college must be an eligible educational institution (including certain vocational schools).

- The credits are available only for qualified tuition and related expenses of an eligible student.

- The credits cannot both be claimed in the same tax year for the same expenses. But each may be claimed for different expenses for different students.

- The income limits are the same.

As for the differences, the taxpayer may claim a Lifetime credit equal to 20 percent of up to $5,000 in qualifying tuition and related expenses. This credit applies to qualified expenses paid by the taxpayer for herself, her spouse, or any dependent. Starting in 2003, the maximum amount of qualified tuition and expenses that may be taken into account in determining the Lifetime credit for a tax year will increase to $10,000. The maximum credit in 2003 will be $2,000 (20% of $10,000). The Lifetime credit (as the name implies) is available to all qualified students, for all qualified education, regardless of whether the education is taken for an advanced degree or not. In addition, there is no limit on the number of years for which the Lifetime credit can be claimed.

INTERACTION WITH COLLEGE SAVINGS ACCOUNTS

Generally speaking, you cannot claim a tax credit or deduction for higher-education expenses that were covered with proceeds from 529 accounts or a Coverdell ESA. This is a complicated subject, governed by ever-shifting rules, so do more research before filing your return.

Resources

WEBSITES

The Motley Fool (www.Fool.com)

Department of Education (www.ed.gov)

College Board (www.collegeboard.com)

SavingforCollege.com (www.savingforcollege.com)

FinAid (www.finaid.org)

FastWeb (www.fastweb.com)

Peterson's (www.petersons.com)

Sallie Mae (www.salliemae.com)

Students.gov (www.students.gov)

WiredScholar (www.wiredscholar.com)

The Scholarship Coach (www.scholarshipcoach.com)

GradSchools.com (www.gradschools.com)

CampusTours.com (www.campustours.com)

Mapping Your Future (www.mapping-your-future.org)

BOOKS

The Best Way to Save for College: A Complete Guide to 529 Plans by Joseph Hurley

Don't Miss Out: The Ambitious Student's Guide to Financial Aid by Anna Leider

The Grad School Handbook: An Insider's Guide to Getting In and Succeeding by Richard Jerrard and Margot Jerrard

How to Go to College Almost for Free by Benjamin Kaplan

Kiplinger's Financing College by Kristin Davis

The Motley Fool Investment Guide for Teens: 8 Steps to Having More Money Than Your Parents Ever Dreamed Of by David Gardner, Tom Gardner, and Selena Maranjian

Paying for College Without Going Broke by Kalman A. Chany

So What Are You Going to Do With That?: A Guide for M.A.'s and Ph.D's Seeking Careers Outside the Academy by Maggie Debelius and Susan Elizabeth Basalla

Index

Page numbers followed by *t* refer to tables.

Vouchers, as funding source, 5

W
West Virginia SMART 529 Plan, 117t
Work-study programs, 68

Also by The Motley Fool